Reiki

Understand Reiki Healing in Under an Hour

(How to Increase and Master Vitality, Improve Your Health and Feel Great)

Paul Navarro

Published By **Bella Frost**

Paul Navarro

Reiki: Understand Reiki Healing in Under an Hour (How to Increase and Master Vitality, Improve Your Health and Feel Great)

ISBN 978-1-9990225-6-3

No part of this guidebook shall be reproduced in any form without permission in writing from the publisher except in the case of brief quotations embodied in critical articles or reviews.

Legal & Disclaimer

The information contained in this book is not designed to replace or take the place of any form of medicine or professional medical advice. The information in this book has been provided for educational & entertainment purposes only.

The information contained in this book has been compiled from sources deemed reliable, and it is accurate to the best of the Author's knowledge; however, the Author cannot guarantee its accuracy and validity and cannot be held liable for any errors or omissions. Changes are periodically made to this book. You must consult your doctor or get professional medical advice before using any of the suggested remedies, techniques, or information in this book.

Upon using the information contained in this book, you agree to hold harmless the Author from and against any damages, costs, and expenses, including any legal fees potentially resulting from the application of any of the information provided by this guide. This disclaimer applies to any damages or injury caused by the use and application, whether directly or indirectly, of any advice or information presented, whether for breach of contract, tort, negligence, personal injury, criminal intent, or under any other cause of action.

You agree to accept all risks of using the information presented inside this book. You need to consult a professional medical practitioner in order to ensure you are both able and healthy enough to participate in this program.

Table Of Contents

Chapter 1: How Reiki Works

REIKI IS a holistic restoration exercise that is based totally at the idea of widespread existence strain strength. All living beings are made from electricity, and this strength can be blocked or stagnant, number one to physical, emotional, or non secular imbalances. By channeling not unusual lifestyles force energy via their hands, Reiki practitioner's goal to get rid of those blockages and sell healing within the body. The concept of installation existence strain power, furthermore called Ki or Qi, is found in plenty of various cultures and recovery traditions. In Reiki, the practitioner acts as a conduit for this electricity, the use of their fingers to direct it to the consumer's frame. Reiki practitioner does now not use their non-public strength, however acts as a channel for the well-known electricity to glide through.

During a Reiki consultation, the patron normally lies down or sits quite definitely even as the practitioner places their fingers on or close to the client's body in a sequence of positions. These positions can also furthermore correspond to particular energy facilities, or chakras, inside the frame, similarly to to regions of tension or pain. The practitioner can also use symbols, mantras, or distinct techniques to enhance the go with the drift of electricity in a few unspecified time in the future of the session. Clients frequently report feeling deeply relaxed and non violent throughout a Reiki session. This rest reaction can useful aid in decreasing physical pressure and tension, fostering peace and well-being. Throughout the session, some customers also can enjoy physical sensations like warmth or tingling wherein the practitioner's fingers are placed.

As Reiki practitioners, we do not forget that getting rid of energy drift limitations improves the body's innate functionality to heal itself. In doing so, it is able to be crucial to cope with physiological imbalances like ache or irritation similarly to emotional and spiritual abnormalities. Although it is regularly combined with conventional medical strategies, reiki is not an opportunity desire to them. Many theories exist concerning how Reiki capabilities. Reiki also can prompt the parasympathetic nerve system, which controls the frame's relaxation reaction, consistent with a few professionals. Some others declare that Reiki may additionally stimulate the body's endorphins, which act as a herbal painkiller. Some declare that Reiki can also have an impact at the energy fields that surround and pervade the recipient on the quantum diploma. Despite the reality that medical experts disagree on how Reiki works, many people assert that they've benefited from the use of it. Although little have a have a take a look at has been executed on the efficacy of Reiki, a few studies have endorsed that it may be beneficial for conditions like pain, anxiety, and depression. Several individuals moreover studies that Reiki can be a beneficial tool for promoting relaxation, lowering anxiety, and improving brand new nicely being. The concept of the overall lifestyles stress strength serves as the foundation for the recuperation technique called reiki. All dwelling things are made from electricity, that could emerge as stagnant or hindered to purpose imbalances on the bodily, emotional, or non secular stages. This is the inspiration upon which Reiki is based totally absolutely without a doubt. Reiki practitioners are looking for to cast off those boundaries and sell recuperation through channeling this energy through their arms.

The particular mechanism via which Reiki works isn't always genuinely understood, however there are several theories that try to deliver an motive at the back of its consequences. Here are some viable reasons for the manner Reiki works:

Energy waft: According to this idea, Reiki acts by way of manner of rebuilding the go with the glide of electricity inside the frame. Reiki practitioners contend that with the useful resource of putting their fingers on or close to a affected individual's body, they're able to use the normal existence stress energy to help easy obstructions and rebalance the frame's power systems. This may additionally inspire healing and relaxation.

Relaxation reaction: It's additionally believed that Reiki reasons the body to loosen up, which could supply an reason behind the way it features. Many instances, customers say they enjoy in particular calm and comfortable at some stage in a Reiki treatment. The frame can revel in lots a whole lot less strain and anxiety in this unstressed circumstance, that can useful aid within the restoration manner.

Mind-body connection: The mind-body connection may be strengthened with Reiki. Reiki can help the frame's innate capability to heal itself with the useful resource of the usage of encouraging rest and lowering stress. This may be in part defined with the useful resource of the deleterious results that strain and anxiety may also have on the immune tool and one among a type frame strategies.

Placebo effect: According to 3 Reiki detractors Reiki has a placebo effect due to which some sufferers receives benefited from a treatment certainly because of the fact they think it will probably be powerful. While the placebo effect may also every so often be at play, many Reiki practitioners and clients report feeling actual advantages from their Reiki intervals that can't be accounted for by means of the usage of the placebo effect by myself.

A holistic recovery technique called reiki makes use of the practitioner's arms to harness traditional life stress strength on the way to inspire recovery and relaxation. Although the proper strategies with the useful resource of which Reiki capabilities aren't simply understood, many people declare to have benefited from using it. People of numerous a while and backgrounds can utilise reiki as a supplemental remedy further to standard medical remedies. With its cognizance on rest, balance, and healing, Reiki has the capability to be a beneficial tool for simply each person searching for to decorate fitness and fitness in their lives.

HOW REIKI DOES NOT WORK

REIKI IS NOT a faith or a shape of voodoo. It is a type of religious remedy that had its beginnings in Japan in the early twentieth century. The exercise is primarily based on the concept that all residing subjects have a existence strain power that may be channeled via a Reiki practitioner's hands to useful resource inside the recipient's restoration and emotional equilibrium. Although Reiki has non secular roots, it isn't related to all of us faith or perception system and can be utilized by the ones of all religions further to the ones who have no religion in any respect.

It's crucial to understand that Reiki is not a magical or superb treatment. Reiki can assist with recovery, balance, and well-being however it cannot take the location of conventional hospital remedy or expert counselling. Reiki ought to be considered as a complementary remedy that aids in the healing approach together with special scientific interventions. It's moreover crucial to hold in mind that the effectiveness of Reiki can also change relying on pretty numerous of factors, inclusive of the affected individual, the practitioner's revel in, and the severity and nature of the infection being treated. The receiver want to be open to the practice, technique it with an open thoughts and coronary heart, and determine to a based studying and strolling towards ordinary so as for Reiki to be effective. Reiki is a adventure of self-discovery and personal growth, and via the use of drawing close to it with a spirit of openness and curiosity, receivers can unfastened up their whole capability and experience the numerous benefits it has to offer.

Reiki is not Law of Attraction. Despite the fact that they'll appear like comparable in positive methods, Reiki and the Law of Attraction are basically particular practices. Reiki is a holistic recuperation method that makes use of power to assist bodily, intellectual, and non secular nicely-being. Reiki practitioners use particular techniques to channel the frame's natural life force energy of the recipient so you can eliminate impediments and sell bodily harmony. On the other hand, the Law of Attraction is a philosophical precept that announces you may take location your goals and pull excellent subjects into your life via the use of manner of specializing in true matters. The Law of Attraction is the concept that similar things appeal to every specific and that you may gather your desires via envisioning and setting forward them. Both Reiki and the Law of Attraction incorporate power and purpose, however their desires and techniques are one-of-a-kind. Reiki focuses on encouraging recovery and neutralizing negativities, whilst the Law of Attraction is targeted on producing precise consequences.

It isn't suggested to apply of Reiki as a tool to strive to persuade or manage your life's sports. Reiki is not a manifestation approach. Instead, it serves as a device to inspire harmony, stability, and health within the frame and mind. Reiki isn't a technique of attracting precise results or tangible subjects into your lifestyles. It can assist to deliver concord, restoration and remarkable energy for your lifestyles. Reiki works with the beneficial resource of helping to easy blockages and sell the natural flow of electricity within the body. This permits the body's herbal healing techniques to function more efficaciously. Reiki can help to sell greater emotional and religious stability thru everyday exercise by the use of lowering stress and tension, and selling a feel of internal peace and nicely-being.

Reiki isn't a manner of directing or controlling sports activities in any manner. The important idea of Reiki exercise is give up, not looking for to direct or have an effect on the flow of frequent energy. If you are attempting to materialize unique results or tangible gadgets in your existence, it might be extra appropriate to look at diverse modalities or practices which are especially designed for this reason. But, if you need to sell more balance, recovery, and well-being in your existence, Reiki may

be a effective and transformative device that will help you in attaining the ones goals.

ORIGIN OF REIKI

REIKI HAS GAINED ground as an opportunity treatment in current years. It is concept to have began in Japan within the early twentieth century; but its unique origins are dubious. The history of the workout is intently associated with the existence of Dr. Mikao Usui, who developed the recovery technique this is now known as Reiki. Dr. Mikao Usui became born inside the Japanese metropolis of Taniai inside the yr 1865. In his quest for records and purpose of existence, he explored a wide style of religious and philosophical traditions from an early age. He spent pretty some time reading approximately the historic Buddhist recuperation practices because he have become so interested by them. Dr. Usui grow to be especially intrigued with the aid of manner of the use of the concept of recuperation through the fingers considering he belief that everyone have become truely able to doing so. He dedicated some years to studying approximately the education and files from the beyond, and in the long run he created a recovery technique he termed Reiki. This technique of remedy became added to Japan with the aid of Dr. Usui and hastily have emerge as well-known there. However, what we recognize approximately the early information of Reiki is primarily based on the memories of his students and fans.

Dr. Chujiro Hayashi, a scholar of Dr. Mikao Usui, achieved a fantastic feature in popularizing Reiki in Japan after which the West. Dr. Hayashi, a clinical medical doctor and military officer, have become stimulated to spread the healing blessings of Reiki to others after in my view experiencing its effectiveness. In the Twenties, he installation a Reiki sanatorium in Tokyo and began out teaching others within the approach.

Hawayo Takata, some different pupil of Dr. Mikao Usui, have become in rate of bringing Reiki to the US. Takata, a Japanese-American woman, became struck thru the usage of the performance of Hayashi's Reiki treatments after receiving them in Japan. Hayashi vast her invitation to visit america to impart Reiki. In the latter half of the 1930s, Hayashi visited america and knowledgeable a pick type of scholars in Hawaii inside the art work of Reiki. One of his students, Takata, later attained the identify of Reiki grasp. She in a while helped unfold Reiki ultimately of the West by means of using coaching thousands of people within the United States and Canada.

Presently, Reiki is one of the most widely used alternative treatment alternatives and is achieved all around the global. The effectiveness of this healing technique is widely recounted and famous, irrespective of the fact that its precise beginnings may be as an alternative difficult to understand. Reiki might be a top notch alternative for you if you need to beautify your sizable properly-being, get rid of strain and anxiety, or heal bodily troubles.

Chapter 2: Indian Roots

THE ALTERNATIVE THERAPY called reiki is perception to have its roots in Japan. Yet, many people assume that India is wherein Reiki originated and that it is an age-antique Indian technique that has been used for a very long time. Indian way of life and spirituality are profoundly ingrained inside the idea of power recovery. All residing topics are perception to be infused with a normal existence pressure power called "Prana" in Hinduism. According to myth, this strength travels through the body through "Nadis," and even as those channels are blocked, it is able to reason bodily and emotional problems.

India's version of electricity therapy, referred to as "Pranic recovery," has been applied for millennia to treatment an entire lot of illnesses. When it involves the use of hand postures and visualization to channel electricity and clean blockages, Pranic restoration strategies are akin to those hired in Reiki. The historical Hindu texts called the Vedas include one of the earliest allusions to the idea of strength recovery in India. These works outline a recovery method referred to as "Ayurveda," this is founded at the mind of enhancing universal fitness and nicely-being even as harmonizing the body's energy.

The workout of yoga had a big impact on the increase of power recuperation in India. Yoga is a holistic area that consists of physical poses, respiratory strategies, and meditation to encourage concord in the frame, mind, and spirit. Yoga is concept to stimulate the drift of Prana through the body and take away obstructions that might be inflicting disease or infection. Several extra power healing modalities, which include chakra restoration and mantra restoration, are practiced in India similarly to yoga and Pranic therapy. The concept in the back of chakra restoration is that the spine carries seven electricity centers, every of which represents a wonderful trouble of the physical, emotional, and non secular self. It is believed that you may attain kingdom of extremely good health and nicely-being by manner of manner of balancing those chakras back into balance.

On the alternative hand, mantra recovery includes repeating holy sounds or phrases to inspire recuperation and balance. This ancient Indian religious exercise has been implemented for millennia to help intellectual, emotional, and religious fitness. There isn't any doubt that it has masses in not unusual with the conventional power recovery approach of the historical Indians. Whether or now not Reiki can be categorized as an Indian artwork, it's far fantastic that it is been profoundly impacted with the useful resource of using the rich non secular and recuperation traditions which have superior in India over hundreds of years. As extra humans appearance to natural and holistic techniques of recovery,

Reiki is now practiced everywhere in the worldwide and is super continuing to advantage reputation. There isn't always any doubt that Reiki has loads to offer people who are ready to find out its numerous advantages, no matter whether or not or no longer or now not you are inquisitive about reading extra approximately the historical Indian roots of this well-known kind of power therapy or certainly searching for to experience its restoration power.

THE PRINCIPLES OF REIKI: THE FIVE PRECEPTS OF DR. MIKAO

THE JAPANESE HEALING approach called reiki is based on the idea of power go together with the glide. It is a holistic method of healing that seeks to harmonize the bodily, mental, and spiritual bodies. The writer of Reiki, Dr. Mikao Usui, created a set of pointers that he taken into consideration important for each non secular and human development. The five precepts of Reiki are those ideas, and they'll be regarded because the cornerstones of the exercising of Reiki.

The 5 precepts of Reiki are:

Just for nowadays, I will now not be irritated

Just for in recent times, I will no longer worry

Just for nowadays, I may be thankful

Just for nowadays, I will do my artwork genuinely

Just for nowadays, I may be type to every dwelling issue

Each of those precepts has a deeper this means that and significance inside the workout of Reiki. Let's find out each principle in more element.

Just for in recent times, I will now not be indignant

This precept emphasizes the significance of developing emotional strength of will and preventing anger from taking on. One can injure oneself and others even as they are angry, it is a sturdy emotion. One can advantage internal peace and concord via letting skip of anger. This precept moreover teaches us to be privy to our mind and emotions and to recognize that they without delay have an impact on our bodily and intellectual properly-being.

Just for nowadays, I will no longer worry

This principle encourages letting bypass of hysteria and worry. Although stressful is a human trait, it may turn out to be crippling if it takes over our lifestyles. One can acquire a country of quiet and tranquilly with the aid of letting flow of fear. This principle also teaches us to stay in the now and to worry much less about the future and extra about what we're able to manipulate.

Just for these days, I might be grateful

This principle teaches us to cultivate thankfulness for all factors of our lives, every huge and insignificant. Gratitude is a robust emotion that has the functionality to make us comfortable and happy. By focused on what we need to be thrilled about, we are able to change our attitude and become extra upbeat and thrilled. This maxim also instills in us a enjoy of gratitude for lifestyles's little pleasures and a revel in of in no way taking a few issue as a right.

Just for nowadays, I will do my artwork absolutely

Being honest and sincere in all aspects of our lives, which includes our art work, is emphasised with the useful resource of this precept. A crucial principle of Reiki is honesty, and it is idea that by being honest, you will improvement spiritually to a greater degree. This principle instructs us to perform our paintings with satisfaction and to the first-rate of our capabilities.

Just for nowadays, I can be type to every dwelling factor

This principle encourages humans to deal with all living topics with love and compassion, together with flora and animals. Being type is a strong force that can decorate our lives and make us happier. By being kind to others, we can begin a extraordinary chain response a great manner to assist genuinely all of us round us in addition to ourselves. This precept also instructs us to be aware about our environmental impact and take the time to stay in concord with the herbal international.

These precepts provide a guide for most important a compassionate, thoughtful life and are supposed to aid practitioners in finding internal harmony, balance, and tranquilly. Reiki practitioners are looking for to treatment both themselves and others through abiding thru method of those mind, similarly to to make the area a more tranquil and loving region. Generally, the five precepts of Reiki inspire humans to allow bypass of horrible emotions like anger and fear, stay within the gift 2nd, unique appreciation, act in reality and kindly, and act with honesty and kindness.

UNDERSTANDING ENERGY: THE CONCEPT OF KI OR QI, AND HOW IT RELATES TO HEALTH AND HEALING.

KI (QI), is one that is shared via many super cultures all over the global. It is regarded as a diffused, life-giving pressure that permeates all dwelling matters and is crucial for preserving bodily, emotional, and spiritual health and fitness. The essential conviction in the importance of this energy endures no matter any variations in terminology and know-how.

Qi in Japanese lifestyle

Qi in Japanese tradition is a key concept in some of disciplines collectively with Reiki, martial arts, and Zen meditation. According to popular perception, it is the existence electricity that permeates all dwelling subjects and can be hired to encourage intellectual, emotional, and non secular healing. In Reiki, practitioners transmit Qi electricity into their patients' our bodies using their arms to manual healing and balance. The concept of Ki permeates many special disciplines, together with martial arts, Zen meditation, and Reiki. All living matters are perception to be infused with qi, that is important for keeping bodily, emotional, and religious fitness and properly being.

Martial arts training are one way Japanese culture emphasizes the fee of Qi. The use of

Ki energy in martial arts like Aikido, Judo, and Karate is emphasized throughout. Qi is employed in the ones strategies to domesticate physical and intellectual region similarly to border and mind manipulate. Practitioners can growth their stability, coordination, and electricity in addition to their experience of calm and focus thru using Qi energy.

Zen meditation is every different awesome software of Qi in Japanese way of life. Zazen, each other name for Zen meditation, is adopting a specific posture at the identical time as sitting and concentrating on the breath. The intention of zazen exercise is to promote inner serenity and readability by the use of supporting practitioners in growing recognition in their mind and emotions. This exercising emphasizes using qi electricity, this is employed via practitioners to hold their posture and keep intellectual focus.

Another instance of the importance of Qi in Japanese life-style is the energy recovery method reiki. In Reiki, practitioners channel Qi power into their patients with their arms, fostering healing and stability. Reiki is based at the idea that blockages or imbalances within the waft of Qi energy reasons infection and ailment, and that with the aid of reestablishing this go along with the float, the frame can treatment itself. Also big in Japanese aesthetics and artwork is using qi strength. For example, the Chado, or Japanese tea rite, locations a strong emphasis on using Qi strength in the course of its rites. Chado includes carefully taking note of each element whilst making and serving tea in a specific way. Chado seeks to set up a connection with the Qi power of the herbal worldwide and to cultivate a experience of interest and appreciation for the splendor and simplicity of the triumphing second. The usage of Qi power may be very often happening in Japanese art work. For instance, the brush is held a sure way at the same time as writing in calligraphy to direct Qi power into the strokes, giving the paintings a revel in of harmony and flow. In traditional Japanese gardens, wherein the region of rocks, timber, and water is meticulously selected to create a enjoy of balance and harmony, the usage of Qi electricity is likewise large.

Chapter 3: Chinese Manner of Lifestyles

Qi in Chinese subculture is a cornerstone of Taoist philosophy, traditional Chinese treatment, and martial arts. According to traditional Chinese remedy, Qi is the existence strain that permeates all living things. A wholesome Qi go with the waft is essential for keeping one's bodily, emotional, and religious nicely-being. Traditional Chinese remedy is one of the maximum essential techniques that Qi is applied in Chinese way of life. Traditional Chinese remedy practitioners rent an entire lot of techniques, which include as acupuncture, natural treatments, and Qi Gong, to stability the body's Qi go together with the waft. In order to stimulate the flow of Qi, skinny needles are inserted into unique frame locations at some stage in acupuncture, whilst natural herbs are utilized in natural remedy to encourage recovery and balance. Qi Gong is a exercising that mixes meditation, moderate movements, and breathing bodily sports to nurture Qi energy and increase health and wellbeing.

Chinese martial arts like Tai Chi and Kung Fu place plenty of significance on qi. Qi is hired in the ones sporting events to hone highbrow focus and energy of will similarly to to boom physical strength, stability, and coordination. Practitioners can enhance their fashionable health and well-being similarly to their ability to shield oneself in conflict via the usage of cultivating Qi electricity.

According to Taoist philosophy, Qi is the life stress that penetrates every component of the cosmos. Taoist teachings kingdom that carrying out a revel in of concord and stability in lifestyles relies upon on the right cultivation and control of Qi strength. Taoist techniques like Qi Gong, Tai Chi, and meditation are intended to domesticate Qi electricity and inspire a experience of concord and internal calm. The importance of Qi electricity is likewise verified in conventional Chinese aesthetics and artwork. For instance, the mind of Qi strength are the muse of the Feng Shui art, which incorporates the placement of devices in a vicinity to encourage harmony and stability. The use of Qi power in Chinese calligraphy is also seen inside the brushstrokes, which can be intended to offer the writing a feel of concord and go along with the go together with the go with the flow. Qi strength is deeply associated with the herbal environment in Chinese lifestyle. The glide of Qi power is strongly associated with the idea of Yin and Yang, which symbolizes the harmony among conflicting forces. The seasons and herbal elements also are taken below attention in conventional Chinese remedy while coping with Qi energy, with numerous methods being employed to balance Qi at diverse intervals of the yr.

Qi in Indian Culture

The idea of Ki power is known as Prana in Indian manner of existence, and it's far perception that Prana is the crucial lifestyles stress that permeates all residing topics. Yoga, Ayurveda, and Tantra are only some of the Indian religious and philosophical systems that every one depend upon Prana. The improvement of Prana power is a critical thing of yoga practice. Practitioners are searching for to balance and enhance the glide of Prana in the end of the frame thru hundreds of respiratory techniques and bodily positions known as Asanas. Achieving physical, emotional, and spiritual well-being is idea to depend upon the right cultivation and manage of Prana.

The concept of Prana is also vital in Ayurveda, an Indian conventional gadget of remedy. Prana must be balanced properly, steady with Ayurvedic practitioners, so you can maintain health and preserve off infection. Prana balance and the promoting of huge health and nicely being are finished through the usage of diverse Ayurveda treatments, which includes rub down, herbal treatment options, and dietary modifications. The non secular and philosophical situation of Tantra, which has its roots in India, locations masses of emphasis on the concept of Prana. Prana power is appeared in Tantra as a powerful stress that can be used to advantage non secular development and transformation. Prana electricity is advanced and directed using masses of techniques, consisting of mantra recitation, visualization, and meditation, if you want to obtain higher geographical areas of recognition. The importance of Prana electricity is also hooked up in numerous styles of Indian art work, collectively with dance, tune, and painting. For instance, in conventional Indian dancing, the emotions and subjects of the dance ought to be conveyed thru the proper cultivation and expression of Prana strength. Similar to this, it is idea that in Indian track, the employment of particular ragas, or musical modes, straight away influences the listener's Prana energy go with the float.

In Indian life-style, the concept of prana is at once associated with the natural environment. All Prana power is idea to originate from the Pancha Bhuta, or five herbal factors. The harmonious interaction of the 5 factors, consistent with Ayurveda, results inside the right balance of Prana, and numerous Ayurvedic treatments are implemented to preserve this balance.

Qi in Native American Culture

The term "Manitou" or "Wakan" refers back to the idea of Qi energy in Native American way of life. It is the conviction that the entirety, living and non-dwelling, possesses an interrelated, interdependent spirit or strength. Its strength permeates the whole thing round us, at the side of the universe and the herbal international. The Native American idea of qi energy is carefully related to each their religious practices and their know-how of nature. Numerous Native American cultures maintain that people need to coexist peacefully with nature because of the fact the natural worldwide is alive and has its non-public spirit. They take into account everything inside the global to be sacred and think that there's a web of lifestyles connecting all matters.

Qi electricity is also a idea this is utilized in Native American recuperation strategies. Traditional healers, commonly known as "remedy guys" or "remedy women," lease an entire lot of strategies to sell healing and restore the body's natural equilibrium. Prayer, chanting, smudging, and the use of medicinal flowers are some examples of these techniques. Restoring the frame's Qi power waft and fostering fashionable nicely being are the dreams. The concept of Qi power is apparent in Native American religious traditions further to recuperation strategies. Rituals and ceremonies are used by many Native American societies to foster spiritual development and conversation with the spirit global. These rituals might also include drumming, creating a track, dancing, and praying. They are frequently finished in sacred locations like mountains, rivers or caves.

Native American paintings and subculture additionally hire the concept of Qi power. Several Native American art traditions, such as weaving, beads, and ceramics, are complete of non secular symbolism. For instance, the Hopi "Kachina" dolls reflect many spirits and energies inside the herbal worldwide, on the identical time due to the fact the Navajo "eye dazzler" sample symbolizes the drift of Ki electricity.

Qi in Native African Culture

Several African cultures and traditions encompass the concept of qi, or energy. Nonetheless, first rate regions and ethnic companies have severa nomenclature and conceptualizations of power. The concept of electricity is proper now associated with nature and the spirits that live there. For example, "Nyama" is a term used to explain the existence stress power that is believed to be found in all residing things in conventional West African faith. It is idea that this strength keeps people wholesome and glad and hyperlinks them to the natural international.

Energy is considered as a lifestyles pressure that flows thru the body and is essential for health in numerous African restoration techniques. For example, the time period "Umoya" refers to the existence pressure strength that flows thru the frame and is in rate of retaining health and strength inside the Zulu subculture of South Africa. Many amazing techniques are regularly utilized in traditional African recuperation practices to encourage the float of energy and reestablish physical equilibrium. Herbal remedies, rubdown, and spiritual healing are a few examples of these techniques. For example, the Yoruba life-style of Nigeria has a way referred to as "Ifa" that makes use of divination and religious steering to apprehend and address contamination.

Many African societies region super significance on tune and dance, which may be additionally belief to be effective approach of interacting with electricity and fostering recuperation. For example, the Senegalese Sufi way of life has a practice referred to as "Zikr" that uses chanting, dancing, and drumming to invoke the divine and foster spiritual restoration.

Qi in Egyptian Culture

Ancient Egyptian civilization isn't often related to the idea of Qi or existence stress electricity. But, the Egyptians did have an concept of electricity that resembles the idea of qi in a few elements. The idea of Ma'at turn out to be vital to historic Egyptian manner of existence. Ma'at, the goddess of justice, reality, and cosmic stability, became reputable because her beliefs had been visible to be important for upholding peace and harmony inside the universe. Ma'at modified into moreover related to a mysterious electricity known as heka, which was notion to have splendid electricity and can be harnessed to regulate the area and impact useful exchange.

Heka turn out to be regularly verified as a serpent or as a stylized photograph of a snake in a coil. The serpent modified into notion to be endowed with magical energy and come to be considered as a signal of renewal and regeneration. Heka come to be moreover related to the power of speech and language, and it changed into idea that precise phrases and spells need to faucet into this strain to deliver specific outcomes. There are a few similarities between the Heka and Qi ideas despite the reality that they will be now not precisely the equal. Heka and Qi are each related to an elusive, mighty pressure that can be used for correct. Both mind also are related to the notions of harmony and stability in the global. However, the unique practices and strategies related to Heka are wonderful from the ones associated with Qi in specific cultures.

Although the idea of Qi is substantially implemented in conventional Eastern medicinal drug and martial arts, it has established hard to research and quantify it using Western scientific strategies. Qi can be related to the electromagnetic fields the body produces, regular with some specialists, no matter the reality that the anxious tool can also be worried. Many practitioners of traditional Chinese remedy and philosophy view the concept of Qi as a critical difficulty of human fitness and strength, no matter the fact that to 3 it can appear esoteric or hard to apprehend. They need to beautify their complete feeling of properly-being through selling stability and harmony in their body, thoughts, and spirit through the usage of Qi.

MEDITATION AND REIKI

ALTHOUGH REIKI IS NOT a form of meditation, it may be used along aspect meditation to beautify properly being and inspire rest. Reiki is an strength healing technique that channels recuperation strength to the affected character using the fingers. In order to direct the electricity to the recipient's frame and encourage bodily, emotional, and religious recuperation, the practitioner adopts quite some hand postures.

On the opportunity hand, meditation is a manner that entails coaching the mind to pay hobby and acquire a deep degree of rest. There are many extremely good styles of meditation, which includes mantra repetition, consciousness, popularity, and visualization.

Although Reiki and meditation are one-of-a-type disciplines, they will be mixed to supply a powerful education that fosters rest, lowers pressure, and improves properly being. Practitioners of Reiki can useful beneficial resource in each physical and emotional restoration through blending it with meditation. Meditation and reiki are two strategies that move well together. Both techniques are imagined to inspire calmness, reduce anxiety, and decorate properly being. These are a few methods Reiki and meditation can complement one another:

Reiki can decorate the meditative u . S .: Reiki can be used to decorate the meditative united states of america via selling rest, lowering pressure and by way of manner of helping to smooth the mind.

Meditation can enhance Reiki: Meditation may be used to decorate Reiki. It helps the practitioner to become greater centered and focused. In turn it permits to increase the effectiveness of Reiki.

Reiki and meditation may be combined: Reiki and meditation can be combined to create a powerful exercising. The practitioner can use Reiki to decorate the meditative nation and make use of the equal to deepen the experience of Reiki.

Both practices sell self-reputation: Both Reiki and meditation sell self-focus and might help the practitioner to grow to be greater in song with their body, thoughts and feelings.

Reiki and meditation can work together to create a effective workout that promotes relaxation, reduces strain, will boom well-being and restoration capacity.

THE STORY

DR. USUI WAS STUDYING and analyzing about non secular practices and restoration techniques, however he have turn out to be nevertheless looking for the solutions. Usui Sensei stumbled for the duration of the ill beggar at the same time as he turned into out for a stroll in a Kyoto community. Dr. Usui halted to speak with the man or woman and inquired about the muse of his disorder. The beggar said that he had lengthy gone severa days without eating and have end up in truth willing.

The beggar received assist from Dr. Usui, who moreover handed him some cash to spend on meals. The beggar expressed gratitude to Usui and inquired as to what Usui may also do in pass lower back. When the beggar turn out to be asked if he knew of any techniques for restoration people, Dr.

Usui said that he turned into searching out a manner to do it. The beggar stated that at the same time as he grow to be blind to any remedies, he had heard of a region called Kurama Yama wherein people may go to discover the this means that of lifestyles. Japan's Mount Kurama Yama is a sacred mountain in Japan.

Intrigued, Dr. Usui made the choice to ascend Kurama Yama, a neighboring mountain, inside the hunt for answers. On the mountain, he fasted and contemplated for 21 days. It end up sooner or later of this time that he had a deep non secular awakening that inspired him to find out Reiki. Dr. Usui's retreat reached its twenty-first day while he had a profound spiritual stumble upon. He skilled a strong electricity surge via his body and seen a fabulous slight descending upon him. He perceived certain symbols and skilled a profound hold near of the cosmos and the manner everything is connected. He perceived a terrific moderate coming into the top of his head and illuminating his complete body with restoration and strength. He understood the important thing to the recuperation that he had been in search of is given as present to him to percent with the sector.

Dr. Usui became so crushed with the aid of his experience that he fell down the mountain, reducing his foot and inflicting it to bleed. He discovered that he must use this power that he had felt at the mountain to help heal himself. He become capable of speedy prevent bleeding. He descended the mountain and made the choice to attempt out his newly found recovery capabilities on a beggar who he frequently noticed with the resource of the temple gates. The beggar declined his offer of food and cash and requested Dr. Usui if he can also help him in finding meaningful employment in its area.

But Dr. Usui understood that certainly giving the beggar meals and coins won't end the man or woman's problems. When the man or woman sat down with the beggar and inquired about his times, he observed that a string of horrible incidents had brought about him to lose his own family, his home, and his source of income. Next, Dr. Usui made the provide to percentage the ideas and techniques he had determined while on Kurama Yama with the beggar, as he changed into confident that Reiki need to assist the person rediscover his revel in of motive and installation a technique of subsistence. The beggar ordinary Dr. Usui's invitation and ended up being his very first student.

According to three memories, the beggar handed away short after coming across Reiki because of the fact he had neglected his physical fitness and was too frail from years spent begging at the streets. According to legend, this incident stronger Dr. Usui's determination to comprise emotional, intellectual, and religious healing into his Reiki exercise and to strain the price of self-care and self-healing in his teachings. Following his come upon, Dr. Usui started out using and education a technique he termed "Reiki" (this means that that "ordinary lifestyles force power"). In order to help people in putting in a connection with the omnipresent life stress strength, Dr. Usui began training and education Reiki and created a machine of attunements. He imparted to his students the symbols he had found in the path of his religious revel in similarly to the hand positions he had used to channel restoration strength. Today's Reiki practitioners although use those symbols to direct their motive and start the go together with the go with the flow of healing strength. His education, which he shared with a huge great form of university college students, ultimately unfold over the globe. Chujiro Hayashi, one in every of his students, went directly to create the technique of hand postures now frequently performed in Reiki treatments.

The story of Dr. Mikao Usui and Mt. Kurama Yama is regularly used to offer an cause at the back of the transformative strength of religious exercise and ability for restoration and boom. This tale acts as a reminder that every so often the answers we attempting to find are proper in front folks, and that it is often through supporting others that we find out our very very personal route.

Chapter 4: What Is Attunement?

EVERY REIKI STUDENT should undergo a Reiki attunement so you will be initiated into or attuned to the Reiki energy and turn out to be a Reiki practitioner. A Reiki Master or teacher frequently plays the attunement manner, which includes a number of ceremonies and procedures to help the scholar hook up with the Reiki electricity and make oneself greater receptive to its go along with the drift.

A meditation or visualization exercising that facilitates to open the pupil's power channels and heighten their sensitivity to strength may be led with the resource of the instructor sooner or later of the Reiki attunement. In order to assist the learner set off their very very own capability to channel this strength, the teacher may even rent unique symbols and hand postures to channel Reiki power into the pupil's frame.

According to legend, receiving an attunement will increase a pupil's sensitivity to strength, turns on their functionality to channel recovery power through their fingers, and strengthens their connection to the lifestyles pressure strength that permeates all dwelling things. Also, it's miles concept to have a purifying and cleaning impact on the body, thoughts, and spirit, helping inside the elimination of obstructions and adverse energies that is probably impeding the scholar's functionality to hook up with the Reiki healing energy.

Once attuned to Reiki, they can use the power to assist others and themselves gain stability, recovery, and relaxation. They can use unique hand motions or symbols to channel the strength, or they may be capable of honestly permit it wash via them even as they recognition their cause on fostering fitness and well-being.

THE REIKI SYMBOLS: THEIR MEANINGS AND USES IN REIKI PRACTICE.

A VITAL ELEMENT of the exercise of Reiki is the usage of symbols, which might be carried out to increase and direct the flow of power for the duration of a Reiki session. Each picture has a unique importance and application this is particular to it, and it is able to be utilized in pretty a few methods to inspire restoration and concord within the body, thoughts, and spirit. The 4 simple Reiki symbols' meanings and packages may be stated on this e-book. During a Reiki session, symbols are hired to attention and manual the energy drift. These symbols may be applied to greater correctly connect to and channel the numerous factors of the huge power that Reiki practitioners art work with thinking about that they're seen representations of these energies.

Moreover, symbols can be used to attain higher states of cognizance and comprehension seeing that they have got a sturdy courting with the unconscious mind. Practitioners can acquire a higher popularity of the strength they may be working with and inspire restoration and balance in both themselves and others thru using Reiki symbols inside the path of meditation or self-healing exercise.

In Reiki, symbols are also employed to facilitate distant recovery via establishing a connection with a person's energy who isn't bodily present. Reiki practitioners can inspire recuperation and balance at some point of time and area by way of visualizing the Reiki image and channeling recuperation electricity inside the route of the character or scenario in need. Symbols deepen the know-how of the common electricity that flows via all living matters and get entry to deeper ranges of attention and expertise.

The Cho Ku Rei Symbol

The Cho Ku Rei sign, moreover referred to as the strength image, is employed to beautify the strength flow throughout a

Reiki session. Also, it aids in the physical recovery manner and gets rid of power blockages. The image, this is generally drawn clockwise, can be applied in some of contexts, which includes visualizing the photo inside the path of meditation or self-healing physical games. It moreover may be placed over part of the body that requires recuperation or ache comfort.

The Sei Hei Ki Symbol

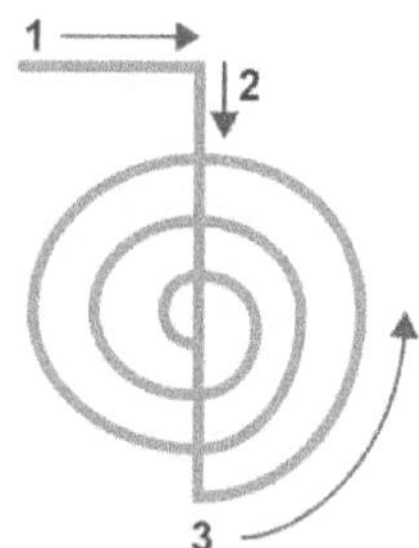

The Sei Hei Ki photograph, moreover known as the intellectual/emotional image, is employed to encourage emotional balance and healing. Moreover, it allows to growth mental interest and clarity. The image, that is generally drawn anticlockwise, may be used in some of contexts, like drawing the sign in the air to take away terrible or stagnant power from a region or location. The photo can be positioned over the forehead or 1/three eye to inspire highbrow clarity and awareness or over the coronary coronary coronary heart to promote emotional healing and stability.

The Hon Sha Ze Sho Nen Symbol

The Hon Sha Ze Sho Nen photograph, moreover called the gap picture, is applied to transmit recuperation power over lengthy distances in each time and area. In order to facilitate distance restoration, it is also carried out to talk with different Reiki practitioners. The image, that is generally drawn clockwise, may be applied in a number of contexts, collectively with: Proving recuperation electricity to someone who isn't always there in individual. Reiki practitioner can ship healing energy to a memory or past event, and sending recovery strength to a goal or destiny occurrence.

The Dai Ko Myo Symbol

The Dai Ko Myo photograph, moreover called the draw close image, is hired to encourage spiritual healing and development. Also, it facilitates communication with one's higher self and advances information of oneself and the cosmos. The picture, that's generally drawn clockwise, may be utilized in some of contexts, which includes: Drawing the sign in the air while meditating or wearing out self-restoration physical sports let you connect to your higher self. Putting the image over your coronary coronary heart can help you expand self-love and popularity.

Several greater symbols, along side the ones for manifestation, safety, and abundance, also are employed in Reiki exercising in addition to the ones four maximum vital ones. Each image has a totally particular importance and application this is unique to it, and it could be applied in plenty of techniques to inspire restoration and harmony within the frame, mind, and spirit.

In cease, Reiki symbols are an essential a part of the practice and are employed all through a Reiki session to beautify and direct the go with the glide of electricity. Each picture has a special importance and application that is particular to it and it may be utilized in quite a few strategies to encourage restoration and harmony within the body, thoughts, and spirit. Reiki practitioners can foster recuperation and concord in each themselves and others with the aid of the usage of the ones symbols to further their consciousness of the electricity that permeates all living topics.

REIKI TRAINING: WHAT IS COVERED AT EACH LEVEL AND WHAT IT ENTAILS?

A JAPANESE HEALING technique referred to as reiki attempts to stability the body's strength to decorate bodily, emotional, and non secular nicely-being. There are commonly 3 levels or stages of reiki schooling, each of which offers college college students a completely particular set of information and capabilities. The 3 unique stages of Reiki education and what they include might be noted in this newsletter.

Level 1 - The Basic Level

Reiki journeys at the primary stage of schooling, now and again referred to as the vital degree. No of your diploma of Reiki schooling or understanding, anybody can get proper of access to this stage. Learning the way to use Reiki to heal self and others is the main goal of Level 1 education. Students observe the vital thoughts of Reiki similarly to its data and mechanics in Level 1. Students moreover test the proper hand positions for treating others further to the way to heal themselves. Students furthermore get their first attunement, that could be a technique for letting Reiki strength go with the flow thru the frame's electricity channels.

At this degree, college college college students advantage the capability to sense power and use it skillfully to spark off relaxation, lower anxiety, and assist in the recuperation of each physical and intellectual illnesses. Reiki can also be used to stability the strength of a constructing, particular items, or possibly specific animals.

Level 2 - The Practitioner Level

For humans who have already completed the number one level of Reiki training and need to in addition their information and application of Reiki, there may be a 2nd degree. The practitioner level is every other name for this degree. Three Reiki symbols are taught to college college college students in Level 2, which permits the recuperation machine and allows the practitioner to attention more cautiously at the emotional and highbrow ranges. The functionality to offer Reiki power to every body or some thing, no matter distance, is every other functionality they growth.

The moral and expert sides of operating in the direction of Reiki also are emphasised in Level 2, consisting of the manner to conduct a consultation, a way to increase a professional rapport with clients, and a manner to price for offerings. Students at this degree will get keep of each other attunement to further increase the go with the flow of Reiki power.

Level 3 - The Master Level

The draw close diploma of Reiki education is the zero.33 and very last degree and is for human beings who have completed the number one stages and need to make bigger their workout or impart Reiki to others. Students are called Reiki masters or instructors at this diploma. The closing photograph utilized in Reiki, the symbol denoting draw near stage, is taught to university students in Level three. Students additionally select out up present day techniques for spiritual increase and energy recovery. This diploma emphasizes the religious issue of Reiki similarly, collectively with self-attention and meditation.

Learning a manner to impart Reiki on others and attune them to it's far the precept aim of Level three. This consists of coming across the way to installation and characteristic a Reiki exercise, the way to attune others to Reiki, and a manner to prepare and lead a Reiki schooling session. Students receive the ultimate attunement at Level three, which strengthens their connection to the Reiki symbols and expands the go together with the float of Reiki energy. This stage is regarded because of the fact the top of Reiki schooling and prepares university students to attune and educate others to Reiki. Graduates of this stage are considered Reiki masters.

Given that Reiki is normally taught through direct transmission from a Reiki Master to a pupil, it would be difficult to offer entire statistics approximately every diploma of training in this ebook. This manner that the learner gets individualized schooling, course, and attunements from the Master and that the education's layout and content material may also variety depending at the trainer and the Reiki lineage they adhere to.

REIKI SELF-TREATMENT: HOW TO PERFORM REIKI ON YOURSELF FOR RELAXATION AND HEALING.

REIKI SELF-TREATMENT MAKES use of power to inspire calmness, lessen anxiety, and help the body's inherent restoration mechanisms. Reiki is a sincere however effective approach of self-care that can be used on oneself.

Chapter 5: Who Can Reiki Help?

NO OF THEIR AGE, gender, faith, or cultural ancient beyond, anyone can benefit from reiki. However it's far critical to maintain in mind that Reiki is a complimentary treatment and should not be implemented in vicinity of sanatorium treatment.

These are some questions to make with the intention to verify whether or no longer Reiki can be splendid for a specific man or woman:

Do you experience any ache or distress to your frame, mind, or spirit?

Have you received a scientific prognosis that is providing you with pain or pain?

Are you willing to try complementary or possibility treatments that will help you manipulate your signs and signs?

Have you ever expert achievement with energy recovery or other comparable treatments?

Are you organized to commit your self to a ordinary Reiki exercise, on the aspect of a sequence of classes, in an effort to obtain the general rewards of the treatment?

It's critical to do not forget that Reiki practitioners should never make diagnoses or advise treatments for illnesses. It's usually fantastic to advise them to are looking for for clinical assistance from an authorized healthcare organization if they may be showing excessive or chronic signs and symptoms. Although reiki can guide health facility treatment, it have to no longer be utilized in region of it.

HOW TO DETERMINE WHETHER A REIKI SESSION IS EFFECTIVE

A SUBTLE ENERGY HEALING TECHNIQUE, reiki works at the bodily, emotional, cerebral, and religious degrees amongst others. Here are a few signs and symptoms that Reiki might be at work inside the course of a consultation:

Relaxation: Deep relaxation is one of the maximum not unusual and direct results of Reiki. Several humans claim to revel in calmness and calmness each in the course of and after a consultation. The calming results of Reiki can useful resource in decreasing bodily strain and tension, improving the excellent of sleep, and fostering feelings of wellknown fitness. The physical body might also additionally experience the calming blessings of Reiki as properly. The introduction of stress hormones like cortisol, that may have lengthy-time period risky effects on the frame, can be decreased at the identical time because the frame is in a deep country of relaxation. Moreover, relaxation can aid recuperation and help the immune device. Reiki can useful resource your fitness whether or now not or not you are in pain bodily or emotionally via growing sense of calmness and well-being. You will sense cushty and relieved of anxiety and pressure.

Warmth or tingling sensations: It is commonplace for people to revel in warmth or tingling sensations during a Reiki session. These feelings are often an instance that the body is responding to the healing energy and that the energy is shifting via its power channels. Different areas of the body also can revel in various stages of warmth or tingling, relying on their severity. While some people can also honestly enjoy moderate warmth or tingling, others could possibly phrase a more potent feeling. Moreover, some oldsters may moreover revel in strain or pulsation.

The warmth or tingling feelings are usually now not uncomfortable and are appeared as a sign that the body is receiving recuperation strength. Moreover, those sensations may also additionally encourage rest and a feeling of nicely being. It's vital to do not forget that no longer each person who receives Reiki will revel in those effects, and that doesn't constantly advise the restoration power isn't always doing its challenge. The effects of Reiki, a slight shape of electricity therapy, might variety from character to character. The recuperation power will hold to art work to stability and harmonize the body's strength systems even if you do no longer experience any warmth or tingling sooner or later of a Reiki consultation.

Release of emotions: During a Reiki session, it's far ordinary for people to enjoy their feelings launch. Reiki can useful useful useful resource inside the launch of energy or blocked emotions that have built up in the body, frequently predominant to the cathartic discharge of emotions that have been held in or repressed. The term "cathartic release of emotions" is a technique wherein a person we should move of repressed feelings or emotions, frequently thru a quick and robust emotional release. It is the technique of letting pass of stored energy or pent-up emotions, which regularly outcomes in a cathartic launch of feelings. Suppressed sentiments or feelings may also additionally moreover come to the floor at some point of a Reiki consultation because the recovery power works to get rid of blockages in the body's electricity structures. Long-repressed feelings can be launched cathartically as a result, which often brings on feelings of treatment or launch. This launch can occur in masses of procedures and variety from man or woman to character. These are some instances of emotions being released at some stage in a Reiki consultation:

Crying: Reiki can help to release feelings which have been held within the frame, often resulting in tears. These tears may be a released as disappointment, grief, or considered one of a type suppressed feelings.

Shaking: The launch of electricity in the course of a Reiki consultation can now and again bring about bodily shaking, which may be a signal that body is freeing power held in the muscular tissues.

Feeling a surprising surge of emotion: Some people may also furthermore experience a stunning surge of emotion all through a Reiki session, together with feeling overwhelmed or experiencing a experience of comfort.

Feeling a enjoy of lightness or launch: The release of feelings at some stage in a Reiki session can often bring about a sense of lightness or launch, as despite the fact that heavy weight is released after being lifted.

It is crucial to go through in thoughts that freeing emotions sooner or later of a Reiki remedy is a everyday and wholesome problem of the recovery method. Pent-up emotions and electricity can help the body heal and accumulate balance. If you do enjoy the discharge of emotions inside the course of a Reiki session, it is vital to permit your self to revel in the feelings completely and to let the system unfold genuinely. This emotional launch is a everyday and healthy detail of the recuperation tool and may guide emotional balance and recovery. In order to make certain that the approach is handled with care and compassion, it is crucial for people to sense cushty and supported at some point of a Reiki consultation, and Reiki practitioners have to have the important education and know-how in operating with emotional launch. It's moreover vital to take into account that no longer all people will enjoy their emotions release inside the route of a Reiki session. The results of Reiki can variety from individual to character, and the restoration strength will feature in the highest high-quality approach for all of us. If you enjoy the discharge of emotions in some unspecified time in the future of a Reiki consultation, it's miles critical so one can permit yourself to revel in the emotions definitely and to allow the way unfold clearly. This will facilitate emotional healing and bring about a sense of rest and release.

Improved sleep: Reiki may be useful for improving sleep in numerous strategies. Firstly, Reiki can assist to reduce stress and anxiety, which can be common reasons of sleep disturbances. Reiki can promote deep relaxation, that can assist to calm the mind and reduce racing mind that may intrude with sleep. Reiki can also assist to stability frame's electricity and sell not unusual properly-being. This permits to guide healthful sleep patterns. When the frame's electricity is balanced and is flowing freely, it promotes better regular health and higher sleep. Hands are positioned in severa procedures in the course of a Reiki consultation, which aids in promoting relaxation and decreasing pressure. Throughout the treatment, the receiver ought to revel in warmth, tingling, or relaxation. Reiki sessions need to be common in case you want to beautify your sleep. Many people discover that they might sleep higher after surely one consultation, however continuing classes can help to keep the benefits and inspire prolonged-time period sleep upgrades.

Reduced pain and infection: Reiki may be useful for lowering ache and infection in numerous ways. Deep relaxation, that can help to lower stress and tension inside the frame, may be advocated by reiki. Pain and pain may be lessened even as the body is cushty.

Reiki can beautify the body's herbal recuperation strategies via balancing the frame's power and fostering popular health. The body's power is greater balanced and unrestricted while this takes area, that would help to reduce infection and enhance famous health. The practitioner have to regularly location their hands in diverse positions on or close to the recipient's frame within the route of a Reiki session, which can useful aid in selling relaxation and reducing pressure. Throughout the treatment, the receiver have to revel in warmth, tingling, or rest. It is crucial to have normal training in order for Reiki to effectively alleviate ache and irritation. Many human beings find out that their ache and infection are decreased after just one session, however continuing periods can assist to maintain the blessings and encourage prolonged-time period discounts in ache and inflammation.

Improved mood: Reiki has diverse advantages for raising mood. First of all, stress and tension, which are common reasons of melancholy and despair, may be lessened through Reiki. Deep relaxation delivered approximately via way of reiki can help to smooth the thoughts and reduce the awful mind that can make one enjoy down. Reiki can encourage more temper and highbrow health by means of way of using balancing the frame's electricity and fostering famous nicely being. It can advantage each bodily and intellectual fitness whilst the body's energy is balanced and freely flowing. Hands are placed in loads of approaches sooner or later of a Reiki session, which may additionally moreover useful resource in selling relaxation and reducing tension. Throughout the treatment, the receiver may additionally need to revel in warmth, tingling, or relaxation.

Reiki periods need to be everyday as a manner to decorate mood. Many people discover that their mood has advanced after truly one consultation, but persevering with education can help to preserve the blessings and encourage lengthy-term temper and emotional properly-being improvements. It is important to apprehend that no longer anyone will experience the equal consequences at some stage in a Reiki consultation, and that the benefits of Reiki might also want to appear regularly and subtly. Also, it is vital to preserve in mind that Reiki is a complimentary therapy and need to no longer be performed in vicinity of hospital treatment. The amazing route of movement is usually to get clinical counsel from a certified healthcare company if you are dealing with severe or continual signs and symptoms and signs.

REIKI SELF-TREATMENT METHOD

STEP 1: Set the Intention

Setting an goal to your desires is important in advance than beginning the Reiki self-remedy. Saying to self, "I want to inspire relaxation and restoration through Reiki," can do that. You consciousness your hobby and direct your energies towards the popular end result through placing an aim.

Step 2: Create a Relaxing Environment

To perform Reiki on your self, it's far critical to create a calming environment. Find a quiet and cushty location in which you can take a seat or lie down. You can dim the lighting fixtures, play some calming tune, and mild candles or incense to create a non violent surroundings.

Step three: Connect with the Energy

The subsequent step is to connect with the Reiki energy. Place your palms over your coronary heart, take a few deep breaths, and recognition your hobby in your breath. Imagine that a heat and loving shiny white coloured energy is flowing into your body with every breath you inhale, and any strain or tension is leaving your frame with each breath you exhale.

Step four: Begin the Self-Treatment

Now don't forget a white light ball soaring above your head. This grouping of energy, or ball of strength, is attached to the time-commemorated life stress strength and is brimming with recuperation energy.

See the white moderate because it regularly strategies the pinnacle of your head. Feel the recovery energy moving into your frame as it touches the pinnacle of your head and movements down your complete body.

Imagine breathing in this white slight energy and permitting it to enter your body with uplifting strength. As you exhale, visualize letting pass of any anxiety, stress, or negativity. Pay interest to any components of your frame which might be stressful or underneath strain. Imagine the strength of white slight pouring into those areas, alleviating the pressure and inspiring relaxation. Spend as a minimum 3 minutes and so long as you choice targeting each vicinity this is strained. Let the strength to go along with the drift through your frame and quiet your mind for as long as you want to even as in this white mild stress-good buy state of affairs.

Step 5: Finish the Self-Treatment

Once the self-remedy is over, take some deep breaths and photo the Reiki strength engulfing your frame. Visualize yourself as healthy, satisfied, and snug. When you are prepared, carefully open your eyes and pause to bear in mind what really occurred.

Step 6: Practice Regularly

This Reiki Self-Treatment may be used on every occasion, everywhere to lessen strain, promote rest, and create a experience of inner peace. With ordinary exercising, you may find out that you feel greater calm, targeted and balanced for your every day life. To enjoy the general advantages of Reiki self-treatment, it's far critical to exercise regularly. Set apart some time each day to connect to the strength and sell rest and recuperation. Even just a few mins an afternoon should make a huge difference to your not unusual nicely-being.

Recommendation

A traditional recommendation among Reiki practitioners is to perform this meditation for 21 right away days. This practice is recommended for some of motives:

Building a dependancy: It takes approximately 21 days to set up a new addiction. By training Reiki for 21 consecutive days, you're more likely to make it a ordinary a part of your everyday.

Balancing energy: Reiki helps to stability the drift of electricity within the body. By walking closer to for 21 days, you supply your body the time it desires to surely modify to the latest energy go with the flow and set up a contemporary experience of balance.

Deepen the exercising: Regular practice of Reiki permits you to deepen your connection with the power and come to be more attuned to its results. By schooling for 21 days, you deliver yourself the opportunity to discover the complete functionality of the workout and deepen your knowledge of it.

Self-healing: Reiki is a powerful tool for self-healing. By working in the direction of for 21 days, you supply yourself the time and place to attention in your private recovery and well-being. This lets in you to revel in the whole blessings of the exercising.

It's critical to phrase that the 21-day practice isn't always a demand for walking in the direction of Reiki, and it is as a exceptional deal as all of us to decide how frequently and for a manner extended they need to practice. The 21-day exercise is without a doubt a recommendation based totally certainly on the benefits that many practitioners have expert.

Some greater guidelines for Reiki self-treatment that permit you to make the maximum of your workout:

Consistency is the important thing: Consistency is the important thing to developing improvement in Reiki. Practicing each day or some instances every week permit you to assemble your energy and gain the desired results.

Quiet and peaceful location: Try to find out a quiet and non violent vicinity wherein you could exercising without any distractions. You also can use candles, aromatherapy, or calming tune to create a relaxing surroundings.

Use Symbols: Reiki symbols will let you to increase the electricity and cognizance in your goal. Use the symbols you had been taught at some point of your Reiki education to beautify yourself-treatment.

Focus on Your Breath: Deep respiration is an powerful way to lighten up and middle your self. Take a few deep breaths before and all through your Reiki self-remedy that will help you hook up with the power and promote relaxation.

Practice Grounding: Grounding allows to stability your power and prevent you from feeling spaced out or ungrounded. You can visualize roots growing out of your feet into the ground or area your hands at the ground to help you experience more grounded.

Trust Your Intuition: As you workout Reiki on your self, be privy to any sensations, emotions, or mind that stand up. Trust your intuition and permit the energy to guide you.

Self-Healing Journal: Keeping a mag of your Reiki self-remedy will assist you to song your progress, set desires and replicate to your reviews. Write down any insights, feelings or sensations which you take a look at for the duration of your workout.

Take Care of Yourself: Reiki self-remedy is a form of self-care, so it is vital to take care of your self in different techniques too. Make positive to get sufficient relaxation, eat healthful components, workout frequently and make wholesome way of lifestyles alternatives that manual your conventional properly-being.

Practice Gratitude: Before and after yourself-remedy, take a 2nd to specific gratitude for the Reiki strength and for your self for taking the time to take deal with your properly-being.

Seek Professional Help: While Reiki may be beneficial in selling rest and healing. It isn't always an alternative to scientific or intellectual treatment. Reiki is a complementary therapy. If you've got had been given any excessive fitness issues or issues, it's miles crucial to are seeking out expert assist.

Chapter 6: Reiki Treatment on Others

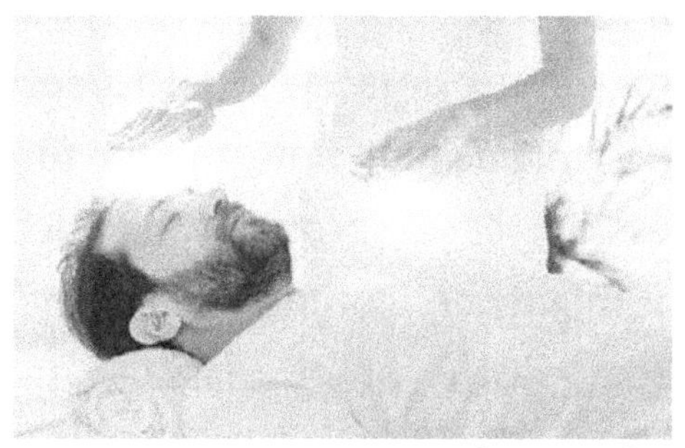

REIKI ENERGY HEALING may be used to deal with others after studying degree 2 Reiki. During a Reiki session, the practitioner uses their hands to channel commonplace existence pressure electricity to the consumer, promoting relaxation, stability, and healing.

Here are some recommendations that is taken into consideration on the same time as performing Reiki treatment on others:

Prepare the Space: Before the patron arrives, the practitioner makes incredible the room is clean and tidy. Some enjoyable music is completed and mild candles or use vital oils are also used to create a relaxing environment.

Explain the Process: Practitioner talks to the consumer approximately what to anticipate in some unspecified time in the future of the session. It is probably defined that patron might be completely clothed and mendacity down on a massage table or sitting in a chair. It might be knowledgeable that practitioner may be placing fingers on or close to their frame to channel energy.

Connect with the Energy: Practitioner takes a few moments to middle self and connect with the Reiki strength earlier than starting the consultation with the useful resource of meditating, visualizing the symbols, or using breath to calm his/her thoughts.

Start at the Head: The practitioner will then start the session on the consumer's head, putting arms on customer's forehead or in the back in their head. Practitioner holds arms in feature for a few minutes, allowing the electricity to glide.

Move Down the Body: Once a place is labored at the top, practitioner movements down the body, setting arms on or near the most strength centers or chakras. Practitioner spends severa minutes on each vicinity, allowing the strength to go with the flow.

Be Mindful of Sensations: As practitioner works on the patron and be aware of any sensations felt in palms or frame. These sensations can provide clues about wherein the consumer can be experiencing blockages or imbalances.

Honor the Client's Boundaries: Reiki is a mild and non-invasive remedy, but it is notwithstanding the truth that vital to honor the client's limitations. If they're uncomfortable with a quality location of the body being touched, the practitioner ought to apprehend their desires and work round it.

Trust the Process: As practitioner works at the customer, they remember the Reiki strength to guide the practitioner. Being in a conduit for the strength is important in choice to controlling or directing it.

End the Session Gracefully: When the consultation is finished, the practitioner gently eliminates fingers and allows the patron to relaxation for a few moments. Practitioner offers the client water or tea and supply a couple of minutes to come back returned another time to senses.

Follow Up: After the consultation, Practitioner follows up with the consumer to see how the consumer is feeling. Practitioner encourages the patron to drink hundreds of water and rest as wanted. It's moreover a first-rate concept to remind them that Reiki is not an possibility to clinical or intellectual remedy and to are looking for expert help if wished.

DISTANCE HEALING WITH REIKI

SENDING Reiki electricity over a distance to someone who is not nearby allows them to enjoy the energy's recuperation homes. Even on the equal time as the recipient isn't bodily gift, distance Reiki can be a strong device for fostering recuperation and rest. You can increase the capability to send Reiki power from a distance and help others in feeling more grounded and balanced with exercise and right reason. Reiki a ways flung healing is an electricity recuperation approach that may be used even though the practitioner and recipient are not bodily present. Although there may be no proof to help it scientifically, many practitioners and users of some distance off Reiki durations record favorable results.

The idea behind distance recuperation is that Reiki energy can be given to all of us, everywhere inside the worldwide, and isn't always confined via time or location. To connect to the recipient and bring recuperation strength to them, the practitioner can lease Reiki symbols, their cause, and visualization techniques. Even despite the fact that it can be hard to image how electricity ought to adventure over a distance, it is essential to keep in thoughts that energy is a vital thing of the universe and can be felt in pretty some techniques. For instance, in spite of the fact that gravity is some difficulty we can not see or sense, we are able to despite the fact that understand its effect on the environment around us. The subtle power of Reiki also may be felt in masses of one of a kind methods, which includes bodily sensations, emotional changes, and religious revelations. Although the effects of Reiki strength won't be measurable in a scientific revel in, many people claim to experience greater comfortable, calm, and centered after receiving Reiki far off restoration. In the give up, someone's beliefs and evaluations may furthermore decide whether or no longer or no longer Reiki far off healing is powerful. Distance recovery may be a sturdy and lifestyles-changing revel in for some human beings, but it can not have masses of an effect on others. It is vital to technique Reiki distance restoration with an open thoughts and a readiness to discover new avenues for recuperation and health, as with every sort of treatment.

REIKI FOR DISEASES/SPECIFIC CONDITIONS

A COMMON COMPLEMENTARY remedy to conventional clinical remedies is reiki, an strength restoration technique. Reiki can aid in promoting relaxation, decreasing anxiety, and helping the body's natural recuperation techniques, however it isn't a substitute for scientific interest. Many psychosomatic illnesses may be cured with reiki. Conditions referred to as psychosomatic ailments are the ones which may be added on by using or made worse with the beneficial useful resource of highbrow elements like strain, worry, or unhappiness. Pain, exhaustion, and digestive troubles are only a few of the bodily signs and symptoms that those illnesses could probably present as. For those who be via psychosomatic ailments, reiki can be a useful supplemental treatment thinking about it is able to ease strain, encourage rest, and decorate emotional properly-being.

Our strength device can emerge as blocked whilst we are below strain or are experiencing one-of-a-kind unpleasant emotions, that could bring about bodily symptoms and contamination. In order to assist the frame's inherent restoration mechanisms and decrease symptoms, Reiki can help to dispose of those blockages and encourage the glide of energy for the duration of the frame. Reiki can aid in freeing emotional blockages and facilitating emotional recuperation in addition to enjoyable and reducing pressure. Unresolved emotional troubles are regularly related to psychosomatic illnesses, and Reiki can sell the discharge of those emotions in a kind and useful way.

Many strategies are used by reiki practitioners to help those who be through psychosomatic ailments. For example, they will attention on fantastic physical electricity regions, like the sun plexus, this is linked to strain and tension. To help the recipient in letting cross of harm emotions and provoking emotional healing, they will furthermore lease visualization sports. For human beings with psychosomatic illnesses, reiki can be a beneficial supplemental treatment. It can decorate emotional properly-being, strain reduction, and relaxation, all of that can useful resource to reduce bodily symptoms and signs and symptoms and symptoms and the body's herbal recovery approaches.

Here are a few times of ways Reiki may be implemented to beneficial resource within the healing of particular illnesses:

Anxiety and Stress: Stress and worry, which can be frequently underlying motives of psychosomatic problems, can be lessened with reiki. It can inspire rest and resource within the frame's launch of tension, that would reduce physical signs and symptoms and signs and symptoms and decorate emotional nicely-being.

Depression: Negative emotions may be released via reiki, that can facilitate emotional healing and decrease depressive symptoms and signs and symptoms. Moreover, it may inspire rest and useful resource in stress discount, every of that could beautify mood and raise emotional well-being.

Chronic Pain: Reiki may be powerful in treating chronic ache via encouraging rest and easing physical anxiety. Release of mental barriers that can be causing bodily signs and signs moreover can be beneficial.

Headaches and Migraines: Reiki can help to reduce the intensity and frequency of complications and migraines thru encouraging rest and easing physical tension. Release of intellectual boundaries that may be causing bodily symptoms and symptoms and symptoms additionally can be beneficial.

Insomnia: Feeling of relaxation and decreased tension, enhances sleep incredible and boom stylish well-being, reiki can be useful in controlling insomnia.

Chronic Fatigue Syndrome: Reiki enables the frame's natural recuperation techniques and encourages rest, that might assist to lessen weariness and growth power. Release of highbrow barriers that can be causing bodily symptoms additionally may be useful.

It is essential to understand that Reiki ought to in no way be carried out in area of traditional medical remedies; instead, it need to generally be utilized further to them. It is critical to attempting to find the advocate of a licensed scientific professional if you are laid low with a specific illness or contamination. As a complementary remedy, reiki can assist help your popular fitness and properly being.

Fibromyalgia: Reiki can help to lessen ache, fatigue and tension related to fibromyalgia. It also can sell relaxation, enhance sleep satisfactory and decorate ordinary properly-being.

Post-stressful pressure disorder (PTSD): In addition to helping with emotional restoration, reiki can also resource with

PTSD signs and symptoms like tension, despair, and insomnia. Also, it could inspire rest and beneficial resource within the launch of highbrow limitations that might be inflicting some of the physical symptoms.

Gastrointestinal problems: Stress and worry can get worse digestion and growth the signs and symptoms and signs and symptoms and symptoms and signs of gastrointestinal ailments like IBS and acid reflux disease sickness. Reiki can help to relieve those signs and symptoms. Also, it can encourage rest and resource in the launch of highbrow barriers that is probably causing some of the physical signs and symptoms and signs and signs and symptoms.

Respiratory situations, together with hypersensitive reactions and hypersensitive reactions: Relaxation and pressure discount introduced about via way of manner of reiki might enhance lung feature and reduce the signs and signs and signs and signs and signs and symptoms of respiration problems. Release of intellectual limitations that can be inflicting physical signs additionally may be beneficial.

Skin conditions, which consist of eczema and psoriasis: Reducing stress and selling calm can help to enhance pores and pores and skin problems and decrease symptoms and symptoms like itching and irritation. Release of mental boundaries that can be inflicting physical signs and symptoms and signs and symptoms additionally may be useful.

Menstrual problems, which incorporates cramps and PMS: In addition to exclusive PMS symptoms and symptoms, reiki can beneficial aid with menstruation pain and cramps. Also, it may inspire relaxation and useful resource within the launch of highbrow barriers that might be inflicting a number of the bodily signs.

High blood pressure: Blood pressure may be dwindled via promoting relaxation and decreasing anxiety, both of which might be facilitated through the use of way of reiki. Release of intellectual obstacles that may be causing physical signs and symptoms can also be useful.

Diabetes: Reiki can be used to decorate huge well-being and encourage rest, that would help to higher regulate blood sugar and lessen diabetes signs and symptoms.

Cancer-related signs and symptoms, which encompass pain and tension: Reiki can assist with emotional healing and ease most cancers remedy element effects like pain, tension, and fatigue. Also, it may inspire relaxation and aid inside the release of highbrow obstacles that is probably inflicting a number of the bodily signs and symptoms.

Addiction and substance abuse: Reiki may be used to facilitate emotional recuperation and to reduce cravings, anxiety, and one in all a kind withdrawal signs associated with substance abuse and addiction. Also, it may encourage relaxation and useful useful resource in the release of intellectual limitations that might be inflicting some of the physical signs and symptoms.

Eating troubles: Reiki may be used to encourage emotional restoration and assist in decreasing eating disease signs such tension, despair, and troubles with frame picture. Also, it is able to encourage rest and useful resource inside the release of intellectual limitations that might be causing a number of the physical signs and symptoms.

Chronic illnesses, which incorporates multiple sclerosis and Parkinson's sickness: Reiki can be used to increase sizable well-being and encourage rest, that could beneficial useful resource in the manipulate of chronic infection symptoms and symptoms and enhance first rate of existence.

Autoimmune illnesses, which encompass rheumatoid arthritis and lupus: Reiki can be used to enhance famous nicely-being and inspire relaxation, which can assist dealing with autoimmune sickness signs and signs and reducing infection.

Reiki have to now not be utilized in place of scientific interest, it's miles important to keep in mind, and sufferers with the ones troubles ought to usually engage with a skilled healthcare organisation to deal with their symptoms and signs and signs and symptoms. Reiki, however, is probably applied as a supplemental remedy to assist fashionable medical methods and enhance tremendous well-being.

Chapter 7: Best Practices for Reiki Practitioners

REIKI PRACTITIONERS SHOULD UPHOLD moral and professional requirements, much like with some other healing treatment, to assure their sufferers' safety and health To defend their clients' protection and well being, reiki practitioners have to work to uphold a high diploma of professionalism and ethical conduct. For Reiki practitioners, the subsequent are a few superb practices:

Boundaries: To create a regular and snug setting, Reiki practitioners want to installation easy limitations with their clients. This includes putting suitable bodily boundaries at some point of the consultation in addition to unambiguous tips for interaction and communique outside of periods.

Confidentiality: Reiki practitioners need to maintain their patients' confidentiality and privateness. This consists of keeping the secrecy of any sensitive information that can be said in the route of the session and now not disclosing non-public information about clients to outsiders with out their permission.

Informed consent: Before beginning a consultation, reiki practitioners must get the patron's knowledgeable consent. This consists of describing the Reiki consultation's purpose, its viable blessings and dangers, and any critical protection measures. Before the session starts offevolved, customers need to have the threat to invite questions and deliver their permission.

Professionalism: Reiki practitioners must conduct themselves professionally always, showing empathy and respect for their sufferers. This consists of upholding ethical thoughts and being open and sincere approximately their credentials, schooling, and revel in.

Self-care: To be capable of provide their customers the greatest care feasible, reiki practitioners have to positioned their personal goals first. This includes undertaking wholesome behaviors for one's frame and thoughts, collectively with regular exercise, a balanced weight loss program, and pressure bargain.

Continuing education: Reiki practitioners want to hold updated at the maximum modern studies and commercial enterprise agency pleasant practices. This involves participating in workshops and continuing schooling commands as well as keeping current-day with developing tendencies inside the enterprise.

Referrals: Where appropriate, reiki practitioners must refer sufferers to certified scientific employees, consisting of while a affected individual wishes a systematic intervention.

BUILDING A REIKI AS PRACTICE AND EARN FROM IT

IT IS feasible to set up a Reiki exercise and make cash from it, however it takes willpower, hard artwork, and a organisation draw near of the Reiki tenets.

The following moves can help you in growing a wealthy Reiki practice:

Being a licensed Reiki practitioner is step one in developing a rich Reiki organization. Each degree of Reiki certification gives you greater in-depth training and records. There are diverse stages. The thriller to mastering Reiki, as with every capability, is workout. Spend time honing your abilities and boosting your self assurance via schooling on each your self and others. Building a a fulfillment Reiki exercise requires networking. Attend nearby holistic sports activities like fairs, workshops, and particular gatherings to network with others and meet feasible clients with wonderful practitioners. Each industrial organisation, together with a Reiki exercise, dreams an excellent net website online. Utilize your internet site to sell your offerings, post Reiki-related facts, and listing your qualifications and facts. Providing specific offers and programs may be a awesome method to increase your customers and develop your business organization. Think about offering specific deals for first-time clients or discounted programs for numerous commands. When acting Reiki, it's important to normally act with professionalism. Always uphold appropriate limits and respect the confidentiality and privateness of your clients. Since reiki is a continuously converting artwork, it is important to decorate your know-how and abilties as a practitioner. Attend workshops and seminars to increase your information and live modern on new strategies. It takes time and artwork to installation a a success Reiki exercise, but with willpower and a love of healing, it's miles viable to have a worthwhile career as a Reiki practitioner.

Reiki has the potential to convert human beings and society in some of techniques. Here are some tactics:

1. Personal transformation: Reiki can help people hook up with their internal selves and get a better expertise of their feelings, mind, and ideals, that could motive non-public transformation. Reiki can assist human beings in freeing emotional blockages, recuperation from beyond traumas, and developing greater effective approximately existence. People may additionally discover a greater experience of reason and clarity about their existence's journey as they turn out to be extra grounded and balanced.

2. Increased empathy and compassion: Reiki can foster compassion and empathy for each oneself and others. People can also moreover turn out to be extra privy to the

interdependence of all residing subjects as they expand a stronger connection to their internal selves. Oneness can be cultivated through reiki, which also can encourage humans to act with empathy and records.

three. Healing the collective: Reiki, via encouraging recuperation on a greater scale, can useful resource in collective transformation. This power can expand to the more community as extra humans hook up with their inner selves and increase in empathy and compassion. Reiki can help in transforming the collective recognition and fostering a extra upbeat, peaceful, and harmonious surroundings through encouraging recuperation and stability.

four. Spiritual boom: Reiki can assist human beings connect with their better selves and expand a better data of their religious journey, that can assist them development spiritually. When human beings experience inner peace, joy, and fulfilment, it could useful useful resource in their non secular increase and evolution.

Reiki has the ability to sell personal and societal transformation by the usage of supporting humans in connecting with their inner selves, fostering empathy and compassion, fostering big-scale recovery, and fostering spiritual increase. Reiki may exchange humans, companies, and the globe through fostering balance, harmony, and recuperation.

I definitely need you have located the data in this ebook on Reiki to be enlightening, motivating, and transformative as we draw to a near. With the usage of the robust approach of reiki, you could access the energy of the universe and use it to enhance your health, concord, and properly-being. Reiki, but, is a lot greater than only a recuperation approach. It is a philosophy that teaches us a way to stay in harmony with nature and increase a sturdy experience of inner tranquilly, love, and compassion. It is a route to higher religious development, a vehicle for personal transformation, and a journey of self-discovery. I strongly propose you to move in advance and further your have a look at of Reiki if you find out yourself inquisitive about the thoughts and techniques noted on this ebook. Reiki has lots to provide, whether or no longer or not you want to cure yourself, help others, or without a doubt come to be extra in detail associated with the power of the universe. But, the Reiki adventure can't be undertaken on one's personal. To comprehend and absolutely maximize its functionality, it needs path, help, and a feel of community. For this cause, I cordially welcome you to embark with me on a voyage of data and exploration as we check out the various methods in which Reiki can improve your existence and uplift your spirit.

You can growth the records, capabilities, and enjoy required to turn out to be a talented and a success Reiki practitioner, capable of direct the universe's energy in effective and transformational strategies, through a methodical software of have a observe and exercise. And even as you examine greater approximately Reiki and located it into exercise, you'll discover that its benefits bypass nicely past the physical plane and useful useful resource in cultivating greater delight, peace, and harmony. I admire you taking the time to have a look at this e-book on Reiki, and I urge you to move ahead collectively together together with your own personal improvement and transformation. Together, we're able to recognize the entire capacity of this effective restoration method and assemble a worldwide this is more non violent and compassionate for actually each person.

Chapter 8: Mindful Eating

Mindfulness is the act of becoming aware of yourself, your mind, frame, and your environment. Mindfulness is a way to ground you inside the truth of now, to calm yourself, and now not lose the instant in the hurry of doing. It without a doubt takes a few moments and a clean exercising, the use of your five senses; assist you to study an smooth method of mindfulness. As a form of self-care, I use a aggregate of mindfulness, Reiki, and crystals to assist with my health.

By tuning into your five senses you could enjoy the now of mindfulness. Ask yourself, "What can I scent? Are there any sensations in my frame to be aware of? What are the noises I pay interest? What does my clothes sense like? Are they tight, unfastened, or comfortable? What do I see around me? Is there a taste in my mouth?" Focusing on your senses is the essential introduction into mindfulness.

I encompass Reiki and crystals to beneficial aid myself in turning into a extra conscious eater. Mindful consuming is being privy to your hunger, the food you will devour, taking the time to scent your food, slowly chewing to taste and useful resource indigestion. Mindful ingesting moreover permits your mind and frame to understand your hunger cues. Eating mindlessly can purpose weight benefit and overeating. Mindful consuming gives you control, so you consume even as you are hungry and save you at the same time as you are whole. It moreover allows you to enjoy the pleasure of consuming and slowing down.

I am a visually oriented individual, so I need a few detail tangible to take me again to the truth to endure in thoughts. Otherwise, I might possibly wander away within the busyness and overlook about. I without a doubt have enlisted crystals and their powers to help me in my goals. I choose to use instinct to select out crystals. If you have a selected want like cravings, cleansing of the kitchen, or weight reduction and are extra comfortable deciding on out crystals based totally on their coloration or meanings; then there's loads of data on-line and in books that would assist you in deciding on out the proper crystal. I pick out out several of my crystals and experience which one has the strongest pull of strength for my dreams.

After cleaning the crystal, you may set it collectively together with your purpose. I use an aim that basically states that I need to be greater aware of my consuming conduct, food intake, to assist with weight reduction and to growth my popular health and nicely-being.

I set the crystal in an opening in my kitchen so that I am privy to it at the same time as cooking. I use Reiki on my meals to infuse them with energy. This moreover allows me time to cut into my starvation and to get pleasure from the smells in preference to mindlessly ingesting.

I even take the crystal grocery shopping. I vicinity it in my pocket. When I arrive at the store, I do a brief self-Reiki with the cause to make smart meals choices and to assist with deciding on out the maximum nutritious food.

Since a part of my cause is focused on fitness and well-being, I moreover use the crystal as a reminder to exercising. In this example, I in reality have the crystal with me on the identical time as I exercising. It evokes me to preserve trying and to do not forget that I in reality have dreams that depend to me, which helps with the instances as soon as I simply don't need to upward thrust up and be energetic.

Overall, this is quite of an smooth manner for me to get a few self-care each day whilst using mindfulness, Reiki, and crystals.

Self Reiki and Art Journaling

One way that I like to apply Reiki is with the useful resource of the use of it as a manual to bring forth inner mind, subconscious troubles, or as a device for a few colour treatment. Sketches, doodles, drawings, pix, or splashes of colour. To exercising this, I would likely recommend which you have a smooth piece of paper and a desire of artwork additives that you can want to use. I'm often attracted to graphite pencils, but I additionally maintain oil pastels and coloured pencils available. I surely have a sketchbook that acts as a seen mag.

Things that you can want:

Colored Pencils

Oil Pastels

Watercolors

Drawing Pencils

Plain paper

Sketchbook

Once you've got were given your workspace installation, reflect onconsideration on an reason for this seen journey. Then at the same time as performing gassho, permit the Reiki to go into you. Think about your reason. Then the usage of the Reiki, carry it to your easy piece of paper and thru the paper. Allow it to be a channel on your Reiki strength.

Essentially, you're infusing the paper with the Reiki energy. Next, you may need to apply the Reiki power on the artwork materials. Sense which components are the ideal ones for you in this day and for this mag paintings. Throughout this seen exploration, I hold to use Reiki to assist pick the following color, pencil, shape, line, or to expose wherein to feature shading or erasures. I moreover permit intuition and Reiki to help me determine even as this visible magazine get admission to is entire for every consultation.

When you are ready to begin, if there are any pictures that have come to then you you could begin drawing that on the paper using whichever pencil, pastel, and many others., you have been attracted to sooner or later of your Reiki intention and meditation. If there can be no particular image which you want to discover, then the usage of your intuition start to doodle. Let the pencil or paint direct your hand. See what bureaucracy, even as you are not actively looking for to make a positive photograph. Let your subconscious come to play on the paper thru the medium, shapes, and features.

What this exercising does, is honestly several topics proper away. The natural act of without a doubt drawing or sketching is relaxing. It draws you into the texture of the paper and the colors which you pick out. This is a shape of mindfulness. Being capable of truely be, in the present, along side your sketchbook and materials. You also can use this as a shape of self-actualization. After you feel that your photo is whole, take a step lower back and have a look at it with clean eyes. What proper away actions you? This isn't always an workout in making paintings. This is the usage of Reiki to help explicit yourself, a manner to peer what's on your mind, to look a seen of your aware and unconscious mind. Do the colors that you have decided on suggest some thing to you? What did you sense while the use of remarkable colorings? Did you choose out to not use colour? Is there a sure feeling or enjoy which you are aware about when you see your caricature? Are the strains and shapes that you have drawn symbolic of a scenario that you're going thru? Were wonderful feelings or thoughts brought out by manner of using superb shapes or movements at the paper? Take some time to consider the way you felt and what you concept at the same time as you have been making this seen magazine access.

I do try to do this weekly. I can find myself drawing for almost an hour. I start without a preconceived notions of the surrender product. I do have a sketchbook that I maintain in particular for this shape of Reiki journaling. Each access is a instance of that day or time. None ever appearance comparable and this usually allows supply me peace of thoughts and clarity of notion.

I want you're capable of revel in trying out this exercise the use of Reki, art work, mindfulness and are rewarded with the delight of making a very particular visible magazine that represents you.

Reiki with Your Intuition

Let's take a look at methods that we increase our instinct with the useful resource of using our Reiki!

First, what's instinct? I don't forget instinct as almost a primal way of our body speakme with itself. Intuition is analyzing to pay attention to cues out of your frame, any feelings or sensations which you might be experiencing, after which to just accept as real with in them.

We so often flip to others to invite for their evaluations and guidance, however we might not pay attention to our very own internal voice. Trust your instinct to be your internal manual.

Have you had that experience while all of a unexpected you simply had this feeling that some element end up approximately to appear, and on your marvel, that instinct emerge as in the long run translated to fact?

When you revel in strongly approximately a few problem that's known as instinct.

It without a doubt isn't right that just a few humans can harness their intuitive powers. Anyone can learn to pay attention to and keep in mind their internal voice. As Reiki practitioners we have the more present of being capable of workout listening and strolling with our intuition via using the usage of the Reiki power to help us.

A every day Reiki session on yourself is the first rate manner to get intune together with your body on an active, physical, and emotional level. This is the important thing to installing a foundation wherein you may construct your accept as true with and take into account in yourself and your intuitive abilties.

Why the need to growth instinct, you ask? Why now not allow your emotional and mental nation be as it is? First and main, intuition promotes top communication. It makes you more sensitive to the people round you; it often keeps you from hurting the ones you adore due to the fact you are intuitive sufficient to understand them.

Intuition additionally makes you an extended manner more innovative than ever. Intuition method freeing extra progressive thoughts for any approach of expression.

Lastly, instinct has a recuperation energy. This healing electricity is not within the physical experience, however in delving deep into your soul to do away with some lousy electricity buried in it. Intuition can stop us from bringing more horrible strength on board. It also can help us recognize on the equal time as it's time to do an aura cleanse or Reiki session. It's all approximately being attentive to yourself.

With that being said, are you prepared to increase your instinct? Here are a few methods to release this present the use of Reiki!

Meditation

Meditating method locating peace in yourself. If your thoughts and coronary coronary heart are cluttered with too much luggage and harm, you wouldn't be capable of calm down that a part of you that could sooner or later initiate intuition.

Let's workout the usage of Reiki along with your meditation. When you meditate, try and do a complete body take a look at. In your thoughts's eye, slowly start out of your head all of the manner for your feet. Stopping to check- in with every body factor and chakra. Assess how each a part of you is feeling in that 2nd.

Now, start once more, at your head, and slowly send Reiki to every body detail and chakra. When I say each a part of your frame, I suggest even your pinnacle eyelids, lower eyelids, the front and back of your chest, each finger in my opinion ... .Stop and offer Reiki to every a part of you. Then re-examine how your entire frame feels and evaluate it to the frame experiment preceding to the Reiki.

Overtime, try and set up a baseline for the way your entire frame feels on the same time as you're in a unbiased putting. This can can help you experience any pings, uncommon sensations, or mind that might pop into your thoughts. Learn a way to pay interest in your frame and "pay attention" your intuition.

Listen

What does this mean? If you are getting ready to making a big selection, permit bypass of all of the inhibitions and head to a quiet area in which you can discover in which letting bypass has added you. Sometimes you simply must pay attention to the voice internal you, and that voice gained't pop out till you permit pass.

Use Reiki to help you get to an area of rest. Let your Reiki guide you into an area of open attention and align your self to your intuition. Ask for Reiki to create a welcoming environment to nourish your intuition and then take delivery of as real with in what you experience, revel in, and suppose.

After letting pass of the inhibitions and all the ones subjects that prevent you from questioning and feeling clearly, by no means count on an answer right away. Give it a touch time, then you definitely definately'll have your answer.

Believe on your first impressions.

When you spot a person for the primary time and count on which you have a proper away information in their core being, opportunities are that effect clearly holds proper. Most of the time, first impressions are delivered by using intuition.

This is in that you really need to learn how to believe in yourself and maintain in mind your intuition. I try to not 2nd wager myself and I tell clients the identical difficulty. There's a cause you had that first affect. It got here to you earlier than you had time to prevent and rationalize it away. It was your inner voice noticing cues and sending you a sign.

Reiki can again help you right here at the side of your first impressions. You can do a quick Reiki take a look at to experience how your strength is interacting with every other. Or, supply Reiki to your self and phrase if you be aware any areas which can be overly touchy. Let the Reiki strength allow you to fulfill your instinct till you attain a stage of comfort in taking note of your first impressions.

Intuition is beneficial, because of the fact on occasion it leads you to some component that cannot be finished in any other case. Decisions are less complicated carried out if armed via this present. Develop intuition now and advantage advantages you could have by no means imagined. Reiki is the kind of fantastic tool in developing your internal communication.

Chapter 9: Slow Down Time

Do you ever enjoy that factor is shifting faster than you understand? That you're whirling and twirling in a vortex of time constraints, records, obligations, and your to-do list. If you may gradual down time then you may have a hazard to re-hobby and re-energize, right?

I definitely have a easy approach of seeking to turn out to be grounded while life feels out of control. Using a aggregate of mindfulness and Reiki, that may be a clean recipe for a quick dose of self-care. This is splendid for any time of the day whilst you just want a few moments of peace and calm.

If you be aware which you are starting to revel in disturbing, concerned, or in case your respiratory is turning into shallow, or any range of your own techniques to recognize that your mind and frame are in need of a time-out. Always listen in your body and it is going to inform you even as it's time to consciousness on your self, that lets in you to get lower back to a experience of groundedness.

First, take some deep belly breaths. Breathe deeply and revel in your stomach enlarge. Don't pressure the enlargement. The diaphragm virtually expands and reasons the stomach to rise on the equal time as you're taking deep, measured breaths.

Next, use a clean mindfulness approach to engage your five senses. Ask your self what you could see, pay attention, odor, taste, and sense. What is something in the the front of you that you can see? Are there loud noises, gentle noises, noises from the out of doors? Are there any particular scents that you may scent? Food, cleaners, flora, or perhaps the fragrance of vehicles. Is there a flavor in your mouth from some detail which you had eaten earlier that day? Can you contact your clothes, a pet, a bit of furniture? Mentally listing your five senses after which see, pay attention, heady scent, taste, and enjoy the sensations which may be right spherical you in that 2d.

The 5 senses exercising lets in to floor you within the gift. Anxiety ought to make you experience out of contact, but taking a 2nd to engage together together with your environment, and incorporating your mind and body, permits you to be inside the second and may ease tension.

After the mindfulness workout , I then take a few minutes to exercise some self-reiki. I suppose it's a genuinely first-rate time for self-reiki. You're already in touch with the sensations of your frame. You're in track together with your mood and you have your vibe set to be aware and awake at this 2nd. This does no longer want to be a whole self-reiki treatment. Just a few moments on some key factors, like crown, brow, throat, coronary heart, belly, and pelvis. A brief treatment for the chakras.

Finally, I cease with a few extra deep belly breaths. Then I can bypass lower back to ordinary life feeling extra energizing, cushty, energized, focused. A bit of deep breathing, mindfulness, and self-reiki is a splendid way to start anew at any factor in the course of your day.

Reiki Healing Messages

There are mornings when I conflict with getting out of bed. The consolation of my mattress room entices me to linger. My legs and arms question me to no longer go with the flow and to now not permit cross of the whole rest. Overnight all of my muscle mass have melted like butter. My dog will revel in that I am stirring, so she will be capable of come over, lick my nose, after which she goes right decrease returned to snoring at my element.

Those are the mornings on the identical time as a small little bit of concept ought to assist me to get up. A little high-quality spark of something to look ahead to when I arise. I need a message from myself. A message that I wrote, with the beneficial beneficial resource of Reiki, to get me connected, centered, aligned, and deliver a bit of colourful restoration to myself.

Enter the concept for growing your non-public bowl of Reiki messages! A lovely bowl of perception and big messages which you yourself crafted. I choice the following permits you to create a way that is all of your personal.

Why a bowl? A bowl is a receptive vessel for holding your thoughts. It allows your hand made messages area to nestle. A bowl permits you ro gain in, shuffle the quantities of paper. It offers enough room, so that you can experience about and intuitively select the message for that second. A bowl is welcoming, the manner it opens up and doesn't constrict. It invitations you to use it as a part of your spiritual adventure.

My bowl for Reiki restoration messages is a vintage Fireware in Peach Lustre , as it's my favored kitchen object. Now, if my husband had decided on the bowl? It might possibly had been a plastic food garage bowl that we had out of place the lid too. Neither manner is right or wrong. We every decided at the vessel we perception changed into the most suitable and useful. Does your bowl want to be special? If you want it to be. It can be a bamboo salad bowl from the thrift hold. Or, it could be a unique heirloom piece. This is not some component that wants to be the focal point. The bowl is high-quality the sector.

My bowl of Reiki inspirational messages is open to my family. They can choose one in the event that they enjoy inquisitive about it. For fun, they may even craft their non-public. Sometimes, collectively, as a totally specific way to bond. Or without a doubt spend time together, related as a circle of relatives, and unconnected to social media.

We write messages collectively. It's almost like a family recreation night. You should begin with a single word and then ask your own family to jot down down down their personal message inspired with the useful resource of that phrase. Or, ask them to do not forget a time they felt happy and ask them to explain the sensations and create a message with their sensory phrases. Ask everybody, "What message of mild, happiness, and idea would in all likelihood you want to study?" and then ask them to leave that message inside the bowl. Maybe they'll pick out their non-public message, or, perhaps, it's going to brighten someone else's day.

Writing can be intimidating. Writing can experience like your mind are being judged. A easy piece of paper can stare at you want a take a look at you forgot approximately. Sometimes, a paper by no means feels the give up of a pen sliding over the grains of fiber.

When you are approximately to jot down down down your messages, try and shake off any anxiety that you could have. This isn't approximately writing like your favored poet. This is about your Reiki, your vibe, your spark of mild. We all have this inner spark of creativity that just desires to be allowed to glide. Your terms can and could heal. Your phrases are the right terms. Let the phrases waft onto the paper. Let the recuperation message pop out and shape onto the net web page. This is your message and it merits to be seen. The inspirational traumatic and loving being which you are is developing phrases to help you channel Reiki.

Before I start to write out my little slips of paper for my Reiki bowl, I do a self restoration Reiki session. For me, it's essential that I'm focused and feeling the energy. I visualize the energy, I enjoy it, after which I close to my eyes and absolutely allow phrases, snap shots, and sensations come to me. I write some component that arises in my mind down onto a bit of paper. This is my start line.

For instance, the opportunity day, after doing my self Reiki, I wrote down the ones words: Recharge, one in each of a type, heal, this second, each day, Now, readability, pleasure, balance, humanity, awe, moderate, fizz, warmth, aware and more.

Then, clearly take a seat down with those terms for a bit. They would possibly spark more terms or mind. Or, attempt definitely writing the simplest phrase down and see if that outcomes in a whole concept or sentence. Take the phrase "Fizz" as an example, it jogs my memory of soda, however it furthermore strikes a chord in my memory of the electrical pulsing of Reiki. I used that word to make a quirky, amusing little poem.

Each day, after I visit my Reiki bowl, I permit my hand to feel the electricity of every message. I use quantities of paper, fold them, and use the texture of electricity and intuition to manual my hand to pick the right message, for me, the proper message, for that moment. It then becomes my pronouncing for the day. I take a seat down with it, reflecting upon its that means in my lifestyles and the greater global. How does, or, how can I use that Reiki message to infuse, encourage, and generate positivity and in addition my religious boom.

The message which you select additionally consists of Reiki strength. It's surely a restoration message. It's a manner to channel a small little little little bit of Reiki and to encourage yourself to generate greater connections on this world thru your Reiki workout.

The Reiki bowl of recovery messages is a personal adventure. It's moreover a fun, revolutionary manner to apply your connection to power and percent it along with your family. I desire your messages deliver you pleasure, peace, recuperation, and connection.

Chapter 10: Full Body Scan

His is a short advent into the exercise of entire body meditation and a manner to pair it to a self-reiki remedy. A complete frame take a look at meditation can final thirty to 40-5 minutes, or you can shorten it relying on your agenda. This shape of meditation lets in you to "see" your frame and to connect with it. Using a entire body take a look at prior and positioned up a self-reiki session additionally lets in you to advantage a better statistics of in which you may require Reiki energy and the way your frame responds to self treatment. Additionally, whilst practiced on a everyday foundation you can advantage the potential to honestly revel in even as your frame is in need. This meditation permits you to gain a deep connection and interest that can later remodel into turning into aware about any physical troubles an awful lot earlier than if you had not practiced this meditation on a ordinary basis.

An entire body check meditation is similar to certainly one of a kind meditation practices, in that, you are attempting to quiet your thoughts, no longer focus on outdoor stimuli, and for bringing about a experience of calmness and clarity. How it differs from special meditation practices is that during desire to searching for to quiet the mind and no longer cognizance on internal thoughts, you can interest in your frame and the sensations that rise up.

To begin, find a snug characteristic to lie down in, ideally in vicinity that is quiet and without vibrant lights or too many outdoor distractions. Close your eyes and attention on the space between your eyes, or your 1/three eye chakra. Take some deep, calm cleansing breaths.

Beginning on the top of your head (or the bottom of your ft, whichever feels right to you), slowly visualize each part of your body and along with your 1/3 eye, journey there. For example, beginning at your crown, you'll visualize the crown of your head. With your mind and your mind's eye, recognition entirely at the crown. What sensations do you enjoy? Hot, bloodless, tingling, humming, peace, calmness....Endless remarkable procedures to pick the phrases for a way this a part of your frame feels. Then journey proper down to your brow. Again, your whole attention is now in your brow. Examine this location alongside side your mind and 1/three eye. Feel the sensations. Eyebrows, then eyelids, ears, cheeks, nose, lips, decrease back of the pinnacle, the neck. You need to use this meditation to examine every a part of your body, for my part. Not the complete head right now, but essential functions each get a save you and go to out of your mind and your thoughts's eye. Imagine it as in spite of the truth that you take stock and want to account for every piece that makes the entire.

Continue proper down to your shoulders, your chest, upper once more, proper upper arm, proper lower arm, wrist, thumb and clearly absolutely everyone finger. Now to the left facet. Moving to your decrease decrease back, hips, proper thigh, right calf, ankle, massive toe, the ft in my view, then the top of the foot and the best. Once you have completed the body experiment, it's time to do it in opposite. If you commenced alongside facet your crown, then now, you can begin collectively together with your ft. Once the alternative body test is down, then take time to revel in the entire body. Feel how all of the distinct factors are affecting the whole and the manner the sensations engage and react.

There shouldn't be a rush or a time constraint to the general body check. Take the time which you need to discover a comfortable tempo. Different factors of your frame can also require more time spent focusing on the sensations. Maybe a few days this workout is quicker than others. There can be one of a kind days in which the calming impact of this full test frame meditation looks like a unique address and you may enjoy the sensation and want to live for a while, and that's surely as quality.

Once you've finished the entire complete frame test, then circulate onto your self-reiki remedy. If you're familiar with the Boysen scanning-that may be a more intimate check that specializes inside the quantities after which the complete. The full body test may give you a deeper belief into in which you would in all likelihood have strength blockages or which organs and the corresponding chakras. See if you may relate what you revel in within the path of the entire body test to the sensations you experience within the path of your self-reiki treatment.

After yourself-reiki remedy, when you have time and sense interested in do some other frame experiment, then achieve this. I often do a far quicker and shortened model with the aid of the use of spending lots a lot much less time at every spot and transferring straight away to the whole frame proper away. I need to take a look at the sooner than and after self-reiki intervals.

I've been working in the path of entire frame scans for a totally long time. I am now capable to inform once I is probably getting ill days earlier than I had earlier than I practiced this meditation. This in truth enables in being able to be proactive in looking for suitable remedies.

Before your subsequent self-reiki consultation try doing a complete body take a look at meditation. See if it's a present day tool for your self care normal. If you are intrigued thru the complete frame check there are various sources on-line and books dedicated to the difficulty.

Breathing through the Chakras

In yogic studies, we research that prana is a familiar life pressure power. Prana surrounds us and whilst we breathe in, we absorb this existence force strength. Breathing bodily games are so essential in yoga, due to the reality they create a mind frame union that also connects us with prana.

Prana additionally exists in the earth and in the solar.

This is an workout that I use in my self reiki exercising to mix breath, meditation, yoga, and chakra rejuvenation. I find this workout to be a beautiful manner to combine all of these recuperation modalities. Breathing sports are so vital in yoga, due to the fact they create a thoughts body union that still connects us with prana.

In yoga, the pose, savasana or corpse pose, you lay in your returned collectively together with your eyes closed. Your palms resting at your element, with either palms raised or down. Your breath is comfortable and you're training slowly breathing in and exhaling. This is a pose of relaxation and simplicity. You can be on this pose for this consultation.

On your next inhale, visualize a white moderate being drawn through you out of your crown chakra. Place your fingertips at the crown of your head and trust this white electricity it really is each prana and reiki, because it enters your crown chakra.

Exhale and visualize the white go with the flow of energy transferring on your 1/3 eye. As you visualize this, circulate your fingertips in your brow. Inhale and preserve to visualize greater white slight lightly flowing into your 1/three eye chakra.

Exhale and now the white slight moves for your throat chakra. Move your fingertips in your throat, except that is uncomfortable then you could do a fingers off reiki function. Inhale, bringing more of this prana and reiki strength to your throat chakra.

Exhale. Your mind movements on your coronary heart chakra, now deliver your fingertips to your coronary heart middle. This white flowing power encases and swirls spherical your coronary heart chakra. Inhale this electricity into your coronary heart chakra.

Exhale and skip your thoughts's eye on your sun plexus chakra. Bring your fingertips on your solar plexus. The white flowing strength is bathing your solar plexus in white mild. Inhale every other breath of this effective healing power.

Exhale and visualize your sacral chakra. Your sacral chakra is shifting freely at the same time as being surrounded with this white flowing energy. Bring your fingertips on your sacral chakra. More energy is surrounding your sacral chakra.

Exhale, the white flowing strength of prana and reiki is shifting all of the way all the way down to your sacral chakra. Now deliver your palms to the sacral chakra. Inhale the flowing power.

Exhale. Now, in your mind's eye, experiment yourself from crown chakra to sacral chakra. Stop at each chakra and visualize it swirling freely with this prana and reiki strength. Lay your arms to your facet and experience your complete body.

This is a powerful combination of numerous restoration modalities and I frequently workout this near bedtime. I desire you are able to contain this into yourself-reiki exercise.

Three Part Breath

This self-care recurring involves a few breathwork referred to as the Three Part Breath. This includes the usage of your whole lungs and respiratory on the same time as visualizing your lung ability. If you're new to the 3 element breath, then you'll want to practice it in steps to understand the 3 precise factors and the manner they sense. Breathing is thru the nose with the mouth closed.

The three thing breath begins inside the lowest a part of your lungs near your diaphragm. You can discuss with it as a belly breath or belly breathing. If sitting circulate-legged is possible for then you definitely skip to that function. Otherwise locate a cushty characteristic that lets in an amazing way to sit down with a proper now lower back. These wearing activities can be done sitting in a pass legend characteristic, sitting in a chair or mendacity down. Note, that the breaths may be professional slightly in another way in a sitting feature as opposed to laying down, so that you could in all likelihood want to grow to be acquainted with how your breath flows at the same time as sitting and then laying down. Otherwise, discover a cushty feature that allows as a way to have a directly decrease again.

Place your fingers onto your belly and near your eyes to pay interest. Draw your belly in the direction of your backbone-this is your exhale. Always begin with an exhale to empty the lungs of stagnant air. On your inhale allow your belly to pinnacle off and exit. Exhale and once more draw your belly in. Inhale and the belly goes out. Your palms to your belly will let you feel the movement and hold a connection in your breath and body. Only your stomach ought to circulate for the duration of this step. Try to work out the inhale and exhale about ten times. Take a stretch ruin earlier than shifting on to the subsequent step.

Sitting in an upright function, you presently will area your palms in your ribcage. Gently squeeze your ribs collectively to your exhale. The squeezing of the ribs isn't completed by way of your palms, but is the movement of your ribcage at the same time as you are focusing in this place. Your palms are definitely placed proper right here that will help you experience the breath. Expand your ribcage on your inhale. Repeat this approximately five times. You ought to reputation for your ribs moving in alignment together with your breath.

The 1/3 a part of the breath is the upper or chest breathing. To exercise, you'll region your hands to your collar bones. Exhaling, you can experience your chest or collar bones start to sink down. Inhaling will permit you to beautify your chest and growth thru your shoulders. Practice this 5 instances.

Eventually, even as you feel that you have each a part of this breath exercise down, then you could incorporate the three steps into one respiration workout. There is not any timetable to feel which you ought to glide directly to the whole breath exercise. Focusing on the man or woman steps can though achieve the notice of deep breathing.

For the complete three element breath exercise, you'll start via exhaling all the air from your lungs. Then inhale, start alongside your stomach breathing, moving to your ribcage, and then your chest respiration. There is a paus at the pinnacle of your inhalation before you begin exhaling. Exhalation starts offevolved with drawing in your stomach, your ribs shifting together and your chest taking region. The complete breath have to appear like this in steps. Draw your stomach in and exhale, allow your stomach out and inhale through your nose, enlarge thru your ribcage and raise your chest. Draw your belly in on the same time as exhaling, ribs flow together and the chest does down.The entire breath ought to be practiced about five times. It's a fluid motion via all of the steps.

I include this with self-reiki with the aid of the use of visualizing a lovely white slight of

Reiki energy getting into my frame with each breath and feeling the white moderate as it cleanses my frame. I draw what I call a white light of Reiki strength down upon me. On my exhale, I recognition on being at peace with this white mild. One my subsequent inhale, I all over again visualize a white mild of strength cascading via my frame filling me with healing, health, and happiness. On my exhale, I attempt to create a moment of stillness with the white light of Reiki power in advance than it actions on. I create a synergy many of the breath movement and the Reiki strength. At the end of every exhale and inhale, I cognizance on the peace that I experience during self-Reiki. I don't use hand positions, due to the truth I visualize the Reiki flowing outside and inside with my breaths, and in this manner it is with out problem accessed for healing.

I need you are able to use this 3 element breath workout together along side your

Reiki workout and that it brings you peace, deep breath recognition, and calm.

Chapter 11: Meditation and Breath for Bedtime

This is my 1/3 article in a sequence concerning self-care. Daily self-reiki is extraordinarily crucial to your well-being. During this pandemic, at the same time as you will in all likelihood discover yourself with greater solitary time than you is probably used to, the equal routine would probably become stagnant. I had been bobbing up with techniques to characteristic some particular strategies of breathwork and meditation to our self-reiki workout. For this text, I will lay out a way of incorporating alternate nose breathing, shade meditation and reiki for a bedtime re(deal with).

Alternate nostril respiratory is a common breathwork practiced in yoga. In Sanskrit, this breathing approach is known as nadi shodhana pranayama and translated refers to a purification go along with the drift. Alternate nostril breathing works at the diffused power body and pairs wonderfully with a self-reiki workout. This is a relaxing breathwork for calming the thoughts, relieving tension and stress. Also, it lets in balance the left and right sides of your thoughts. It's terrific at bedtime.

To workout trade respiration, take a seat down in a comfortable feature. First, convey the thumb of your left hand on your left nose and close to that nose. Exhale via your proper nostril. Before your inhalation there may be a slight pause, and then you inhale through the right nostril. Release your left nostril and the usage of the ring finger of your left hand, now close to your right nostril. Exhale through your left nostril, pause, then inhale thru your left nose. Switch elements via bringing your thumb once more to shut your left nose and releasing your ring finger from the proper nose. Essentially, it's far an exhale/inhale on one detail, you cannot be breathing in and exhaling that identical breath from one nostril. Repeat for approximately five to 10 cycles. Contraindications for trade nostril respiration are; if you have a cold, sinus infection, allergic reactions or different respiratory troubles.

Some nights, I take a look at the change respiratory with a color meditation. You can stay inside the identical role or lay down for this meditation. Your breath returns to regular, close your eyes. Using your thoughts's eye, allow a colour come to you. In this example, I will use purple. Envision a huge pink swirl or orb in front of you. Focus on this color. Watch it go along with the float, deepen after which get lighter. Your coloration should possibly even start to change. Perhaps it's now blue. The colour is always a recovery shade. Your mind's eye is only focused on the coloration. Continue breathing via your nose with deep breaths that make bigger your belly. Next, visualize the air because the shade and breath in it. Allow this recuperation color, red in this situation, to go with the flow thru your body. On your exhale, breathe out this shade. I often use this colour meditation as an intuitive way to let my mind's eye or subconscious tell me what chakra could possibly want to be centered on in the course of my self-reiki. Continue visualizing the coloration and breathing it outside and inside.

When you are prepared, the ultimate step on this bedtime ritual is yourself-reiki workout. At this element, I'm normally already efficaciously in bed. Allow your self-reiki exercising to hold via bringing in the recuperation reiki strength and the use of your arms to heal your self.

I preference this aids you in a restful sleep.

Reiki for Your Family

Thrift Shopping

Do you like going thrift buying? Do you need looking through the collection of donated devices? Maybe antique vibes enchantment to you. Or, possibly you're a Mid Century Modern aficionado.

Thrift purchasing is an extraordinary way to keep coins and additionally to lessen the amount of waste because of rapid fashion and hold gadgets out of landfills.

Have you ever located that on the equal time as you're at the second one hand save, a few devices name to you? Maybe you've observed that gadgets you had disregarded a second in advance than are surely catching your eye? Or is there an item that makes you enjoy a horrible sensation?

Psychometry is the capability to accumulate statistics from inanimate objects. This records might probably pertain to how the item had been previously used. Or, you would probably verify belief into the previous owner. As a reiki practitioner you can find out your self choosing up doodads on the thrift preserve and getting a revel in, or feeling, about the object. Psychometry is an exercising in using your intuitive insight collectively with your ability to apprehend from throughout the veil.

You can use reiki that will help you find out devices that resonate with you at the side of psychometry. If you have got ever long past shopping for a crystal, and used your fingers to manual you till you got a tingle that felt proper, then you definitely without a doubt're acquainted with the approach. For instance, allow's say you discover an antique pair of timber cube which you fancy. However, you genuinely aren't quite wonderful if the power you are sensing is right for you. Open your self as lots as receiving reiki after which use your arms, slightly above the object, in this case dice, to allow pics or sensations to skip over to you. Are you sensing any story or thoughts that sense out of doors of yourself and not your very very very own? You might be selecting up on residual energies.

Now, allow's say that you determined the cube had been proper for you. You may moreover want to buy them but you don't constantly want the residual electricity of the preceding owner to live attached to the cube.

In that case, then you definitely definately use reiki to help you reduce the cords for your new buy. Drawing the photo Cho Ku Rei, or visualizing it, Choku Rei facilitates direct energy and gives motive to this power. Visualize the reiki power filling up the cube (or one in every of a kind object) and starting up the strength to your destiny intended purposes.

Thrift shopping for and reiki circulate hand in hand. You love the thrill of looking for gadgets which have been previously used, need to reduce your effect on Earth and save cash. Reiki will will let you deliver a cutting-edge-day lively lifestyles and clean 2nd hand devices of stagnant or undesirable energies. Second hand gadgets however, way to reiki, much like new to you!

Staying Cool inside the Heat

Tips for Staying Cool within the Heat with Reiki

It is rather heat in which I live. The heat is zapping our strength and leaving us tired. So, I try to use my Reiki recurring and change it according with the seasonal shifts. In this intense heat, I try to channel Reiki strength into helping make my own family and I more cushty. These are a number of the guidelines I use in the route of the summer season.

Have ice cube trays? I'm type of vintage college, so we don't have a fridge that makes ice. So, I make the photo Choku Rei (or any Reiki photograph you need to) into every compartment of the tray, add the water, and then assume it to freeze. Later, I then have a chilly drink infused with ice cold Reiki.

You can freeze aloe vera gel in an ice dice tray too. Repeat the stairs above, besides this time the icy cold Reiki is infused inside the healing homes of aloe and may soothe your sunburnt pores and skin.

Speaking of ice, is there condensation at the glass of your bloodless drink? If so, then that's a few different way to apply Reiki. Draw the symbols into the condensation at the out of doors of your glass.

Do you locate yourself making lemonade, sweet tea, or any drink in which you can add sugar? Try tracing any of the Reiki symbols into the sugar. Then stir it into your liquid.

Are you not using the oven and range as an entire lot a good way to keep the warm temperature out of your kitchen? Do you find out your self cooking greater outdoorsy sorts of elements like barbecue or grilling? Summer additives ring a bell in me of condiments. Condiments are an clean manner to write down down the symbols onto your food. Put a Choku Rei ketchup photo (or any Reiki picture you want to) to your roll.

Going outdoor in the sun and approximately to put on some sunscreen for protection? I even have ideas that you can try with sunscreen and Reiki. First, look at the sunscreen and draw the Reiki symbols onto your body before rubbing it into your pores and pores and skin. Second, attempt doing a short self Reiki consultation the use of your sunscreen software as a manner to transport through your intuitive hand positions. For example, are you approximately to put sunscreen on your fingers? Then channel Reiki to that region too!

Do you've got the posh of swimming, both in a pool, creek, or ocean? Have you ever tried to channel Reiki will in the water? I surely locate it pretty tough. It's a exercise in attention, visualization, and sensation. The water will trade your perception of the way you experience the Reiki. Adding the detail of water on the identical time as doing a self Reiki treatment is some component that I regularly exercise due to the fact it's so difficult for me. Use the cooling blessings of the water to interact your exercising!

Make use of the temperature range at some stage in your day. Can you turn up your self-care everyday to the early mornings, earlier than the most updated part of the day. Or, are you capable of find out a quiet spot, outdoor at night time time, and practice inside the cooling consequences of moonlight?

Try a visualization approach of being in an area this is cool, calm, and breezy. Or find out a guided meditation that takes you on a adventure to a cooler locale. If you can't physical be a laugh at the seaside then you could sincerely use your meditative time to take you there.

Experience deep gratitude for the surprising shifts in climate. Is there a thunderstorm coming? Try channeling that energy and the use of Reiki at some point of the typhoon. Acknowledge the significance of the climate shift in cooling down the earth spherical you. Experience the rain as an energy and vibration.

Keep your Reiki intervals shorter than regular. Take extra breaks and permit yourself to settle down. Consider your Reiki routine inside the path of the summer season, can you are making it greater aim unique? Channel Reiki to help alleviate your response to the warmth.

Once the sun has lengthy beyond down, see if you may sit and watch the vegetation and fauna that becomes lively in the meantime. Dusk is a wonderful time, while the air is cooling down and there's plenty wild hobby round. Try to share Reiki with the animals. Even in an town putting, there's loads of herbal world at night time, see if they're inquisitive about receiving any Reiki strength. Allow yourself the attraction on time outdoor within the coolness of the night time with simply Reiki and the wild through your aspect.

Good Night Hug

Sometimes, at night time, as I'm laying right all the manner all the way down to sleep, I ship my family a hug the usage of Reiki. There's no bodily touching, nor are there hand positions. I use visualization, intention, and affirmation to ensconce them in a shielding bubble full of Reiki and some elemental power.

Here is the approach that I use, in a grade by grade format. To begin, I am already laying down in bed, moments, in advance than I nod off. I visualize what my body looks as if, as despite the fact that being taken into consideration from above. Then, I experience the relationship that my body has to the bed to help keep me grounded.

Next, I believe power coming through me, proper down to the ground, and persevering with past until it connects to the Earth. I view it as tendrils of shifting strength much like little fairy lighting. The next step is that I visualize energy from my body going up within the route of the Sky. It appears precisely just like the strength connecting me to the Earth.

Through these connections, Earth To Sky, there may be a regular movement of strength. I visualize it assembly at my center or Solar Plexus Chakra. At that aspect, I visualize a white mild stepping into me and ask that Reiki begin channeling via me. As the Reiki enters through the Crown Chakra and makes its way to the Solar Plexus Chakra, it meets with the Earth and Sky power.

It's a effective aggregate that consequences at the same time as the basic energies of Earth and Sky meet the Reiki power. There's a powerful colorful mild, like a celebrity illuminating the night time time. These energies, together, then start to waft outwards via my finger guidelines. I ask that it visit each of my own family individuals (all of us stay collectively, so there's no distance involved. Also, my canine is included as a member of the family).

I visualize those tendrils of electricity reaching my own family. We all turn out to be interconnected like a web. The energies are although in everyday movement and begin to transport in a round style. The circular movement blooms and we every are then blanketed thru a sphere, which looks like a bubble. We every have our very personal sphere, but are even though associated with the tendrils of electricity.

It's at this thing that I ask the Reiki to are seeking out every family member and assist them for their maximum appropriate. I ask that each of us have a restful sleep and that we'd huge conscious refreshed and renewed. I hold channeling the power for a few moments. Then, I visualize the spheres dissolving. Slowly, the tendrils of strength retract from every family member. I ship the energy decrease returned to the Earth. I send the strength decrease once more to the Sky. Then I visualize the Reiki strength being launched thru the soles of my toes. Finally, I thank the Universe for allowing me to channel Reiki, Earth and Sky.

It's in this manner that I am in a function to connect to my family, one final time, in advance than all people go together with the go together with the glide off to our night-time dream filled journeys.

Chapter 12: Family Box Project

This past month, I started out a project for my family that I've been making plans for some time. I gave each folks a unique field, slips of paper, pen, and defined a Reiki Box's purpose. Then every parents have come to be allowed to write down down some element that we favored to get maintain of Reiki electricity. Such as, non-public goals, sports, intentions, desires, or awesome human beings.

My private Reiki Box is timber with a huge brass inlay regular like a coronary coronary heart. I knew I favored Reiki bins for my husband and son and preferred the containers to have a concord of format. I placed a massive wood coronary coronary coronary heart shaped field for my son at a thrift store. Months later, I came about upon a coronary heart usual area product of soapstone with an inlay of mother of pearl. Once I had determined three containers, all with a coronary heart motif, and every unique enough to represent our individual personalities, I commenced the Reiki Box Project.

My Reiki teacher gave each of her university college students a chunk of Icelandic Spar to location in our Reiki boxes. She stated that this crystal grow to be used for targeted strength and turn out to be exceptional for putting in with our paper intentions. I placed portions of Icelandic Spar in every of our packing containers.

Then I allow my husband and son apprehend that the boxes have been prepared and they positioned their slips of paper internal. Additionally, I've placed quantities of paper with Choku Rei, Sei He Ki, Hon Sha Ze Sho Nen and Dai Ko Myo. I reiki the containers normal. I use reiki strength on every field in my opinion and then stack them one on top of every brilliant and use reiki on all three at the same time.

I haven't observe any of their slips of paper, a brilliant manner to feel steady in records that their requests are private and private. I do ask, as quickly as every week, in the occasion that they need to make any changes or updates.

So far, the comments has been in fact fantastic. My husband stated, "Wow, matters are truely taking vicinity and I realize it's that Reiki Box. It's simply too much of a twist of fate that every one of these items have began out taking place after I positioned my piece of paper in the container. I can experience the power and it's pretty first rate."

Help with Homesickness

Another manner we use Reiki to assist alleviate homesickness is with the useful resource of way of sending postcards. I Reiki every card with a message of affection and then an actual written message that's usually tremendously comical. My son is aware that I even have used Reiki at the postcards and it's an additional manner to help him exercise self-care and self-Reiki.

When he comes all over again from camp, we speak the far off recuperation. He we may additionally need to me apprehend if he felt or obtained any messages. Often, clearly information that I became sending it at a advantageous time, is sort of a hug that he feels every day even as a long way from domestic.

Personally, sending Reiki thru faraway recovery has been noticeably useful for us in assisting with homesickness. My son thoroughly enjoys camp and I understand that this has helped him together along along with his misgivings approximately leaving for per week and being without his dad and mom.

Homeschooling and Reiki

While homeschooling our son become generally going to be our preference for his schooling, I didn't understand how hundreds I would enjoy the time that I in truth have at home. I've constantly cherished analyzing and mastering. While my son sits and works at his faculty, I clearly have used this time to further my information and skills of Reiki. I really have a properly-stocked library full of books on Reiki and other energy healing modalities.

I love that my son can see that on the equal time as an person you may although increase their horizon, that there's in no manner an surrender to getting to know (if one wishes). That to have a perceive of Master doesn't endorse there's an give up line. Mastering is a lifelong method.

Much like my son has projects and homework, I actually have specific Reiki strategies that I need to work on. He's always willing to assist me with my work, and I, with him. When I offered a Tibetan creating a track bowl, he have become the number one one to exercising the use of it.

We watched a video on the generation and physics within the returned of the bowls. Then he patiently allowed me to apply it in some unspecified time in the future of a Reiki session.

He constantly gives comments – similar to I provide pointers together together with his Crystal Reiki opened a new avenue for joint studying. He has generally cherished rocks, minerals, and gem stones. We have prolonged beyond to many gem/mineral suggests together and every preserve for what we'd like for our person collections. With the Crystal Reiki, we used it as an opportunity to observe new facts about crystals, their form, shape, characteristic and to share what we every already knew.

We from time to time use coloration remedy and Reiki as our shape of artwork. We have journals and use this as a method to permit our instinct, electricity, and subconscious free and use distinct mediums to create visible portions.

Reiki has given him extra assist for on the identical time as he is annoying approximately a check or challenge. Deep respiratory, meditation, and critical oils haven't had too much of a relaxing effect on his anxieties. However, a short Reiki consultation appears to help him cognizance, kick back out, and end up focused at the project.

We've both come to revel in our homeschooling enjoy greater now that we've partnered it with Reiki.

Reiki for Your Friends

Sleep Sachet

I currently had a client that became having problem in falling asleep.

Chapter 13: Write Your Own Meditation Scripts

You can create your very very own Reiki meditation script to use for yourself, your friends, or customers.

You can infuse your meditation with Reiki on the same time as writing it or ship Reiki out to those which may be present. Charge your phrases with the strength that is Reiki. If you are doing an in man or woman meditation then you could float approximately the room and supply mini Reiki healing, or, do all and sundry in the room in the end of the consultation.

First, pick out the intention of your meditation. Is it for rest, to help useful aid in sleep, or to calm anxiety? Meditation scripts are surely short reminiscences, so you need to ensure which you are staying on detail with a normal message. If your intention is to apply this meditation for relaxation then you'll want to create your script across the concept of relaxation.

Then it's time in your setting. Using the instance of rest, reflect onconsideration on locations that lighten up you (or, are maximum normally concept of as fun). Such as a quiet seashore, a meadow, or sitting underneath a tree. Using phrases create this putting so that you can surely visualize the scene.

Use your five senses that will help you with the placing. If you're at a quiet beach, what are you capable of pay attention? Waves, gulls, or perhaps the flapping of your umbrella? Can you revel in the sand? Describe the sand to make your meditation actually expressive. Is there a breeze, would it not make you experience cool or comforted? How exquisite is the sun? Are there clouds? I as soon as participated in a meditation that gave out little bits of sunscreen for us to apply as hand lotion. The setting changed into the seashore and the manual desired us to odor the revel in. You really need to apply descriptive words to create a script that paints an picture of what you note in your mind's eye.

To start your meditation, you need to apply a respiration workout to assist with grounding, centering and focusing on the meditation. Allow pauses to your speech for the ones paying attention to your meditation to observe your steering. If you ask them to area quite surely, pause and allow the time to perform that. You don't need all of us feeling like they omitted a number of the meditation due to the fact they had been transferring around.

Then your script need to turn decrease once more for your essential message. Uplifting and inspirational phrases that assist instill a feel of rest. Que participants to revel in their our bodies a laugh and to find out the muscles in this state. Ask them to breathe deeper. This is the majority of your meditation script so explore the amazing procedures that you could create a holistic whole frame enjoy of your goal for this experience.

When you are nearing the give up of your script you need to slowly deliver lower lower back those which can be meditating. Let them slowly sense their actual surroundings. Ask them to softly deliver recognition and movement to their toes and hands. You want to create a clean awakening decrease decrease again to the immediately of now.

Writing a script is like writing a tale. There's a subject, a placing, a message and descriptive terms. There's loads of opportunity in a script with the goal to show off your particular Reiki abilties.

Reiki Infused Plant Essences

You is probably familiar with flower essences. These are made thru the usage of putting plant life, lightly, into a bowl of water and allowing their vibrational essence to infuse the water. The flora are then eliminated and the water that remains is considered the mom tincture. The mom tincture is then diluted and combined with a preservative (each alcohol or non-alcoholic liquid including vinegar). Then via numerous dilutions of the mother tincture, a dosage bottle is created.

Flower essences are a vibrational medication which might be presupposed to help with emotions and mind. As a vibrational recovery method, flower essences paintings on a person's lively and ethereal our our our bodies.

Without the use of the real flora, Reiki practitioners can use Reiki power to attune themselves to the vegetation and make essences primarily based completely on the vibrational signature. You can attune your self to a flower, through looking at an photograph of it on line, with the resource of using reading and expertise approximately its shape, feature, and metaphysical traits. For example, you can find an image of a rose, then take time to take a look at about roses, just so you have emerge as familiar with them as an lively being and they'll be no longer a stranger, you may then draw a rose onto a chunk of paper (non-compulsory), and then pass back to the picture of the rose. Open up your coronary coronary heart and thoughts to the rose, the records you've got were given placed on line, and ask to be attuned to the electricity of Rose (this may be the archetypal discern for all roses and not actually one rose plant) you may be growing an open lively pathway using Reiki electricity to hook up with the Rose's (for this example) lively and vibrational nature.

You also can attune yourself to any flower that you find in a public garden or out of doors. This is a incredible exercising, specifically if, like me, you live in a town with confined get right of entry to to flora and plants.

There are many books and internet web sites on line that can help you recognize the way to use flower essences and for which emotion or thoughts they correspond to. This is treasured facts even as you need to start attuning yourself to plant life and making your personal Reiki flower essences.

In conventional flower essences you may start with the mom tincture. However, with this method, you don't need to have tinctures or dosage bottles stored within the refrigerator. Instead, you can infuse your consuming water with the Reiki flower essence on an as desired foundation. By attuning yourself to the brilliant vegetation, you're able to name upon them at the same time as no longer having to count on the proper season, or, having to discover and order the right essences. You can create your very very own vibrational essences as soon as you have recognized the flowers vibrational signature and attuned your self to its energy.